Great Religions of the Holy Land

An Historical Guide to Sacred Places and Sites

Stuart E. Rosenberg

Published By
ORBOOKS
P.O. BOX 12
Postal Stn. T—Toronto 19, Canada

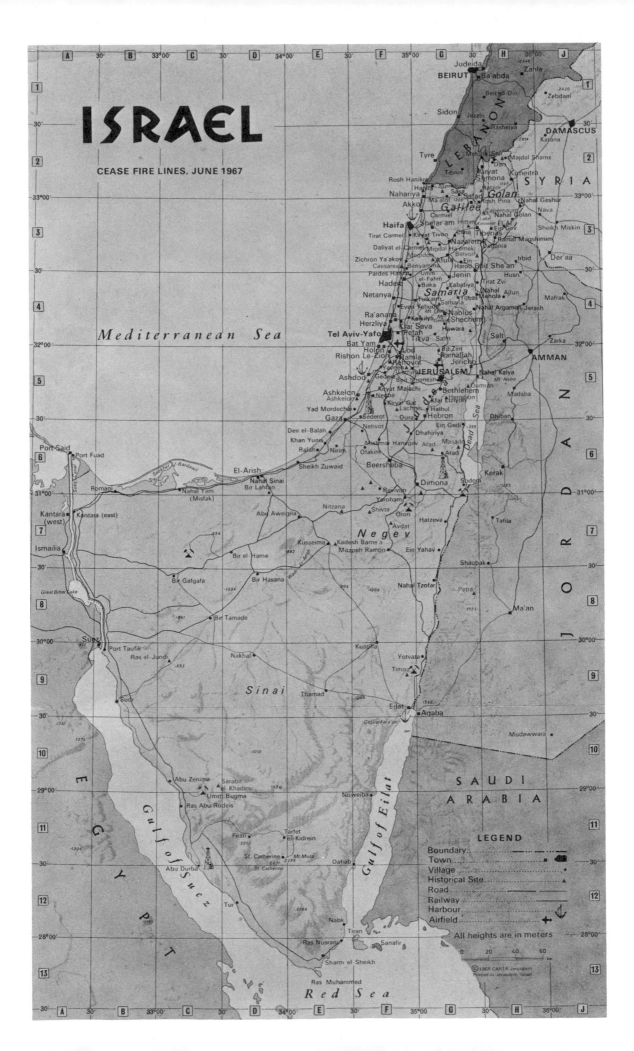

ISRAEL

CEASE FIRE LINES, JUNE 1967

LEGEND

Boundary	
Town	
Village	
Historical Site	
Road	
Railway	
Harbour	
Airfield	

All heights are in meters

0   20   40   60
km

© 1968 CARTA Jerusalem
Printed in Jerusalem, Israel

INDEX TO MAP

Library of Congress Catalogue
Number: 70-159839

Printed and Bound in Canada
ISBN—O—919580-00-9
Published By ORBOOKS
P.O. BOX 12
Postal Stn. T — Toronto 19, Canada

. . . Majestic Jerusalem

This book is reverently dedicated to pilgrims of all faiths

Contents

Dates to Remember

BIBLICAL PERIOD 1850-445 B.C.
The Patriarchs: Abraham, Isaac, and Jacob   c. 1850-1700 B.C.
The Exodus and the Conquest of Canaan   c.1300-1200 B.C.
The Judges: Deborah, Gideon, Samson   c. 1200-1020 B.C.
Israel's First King: Saul   c. 1020 B.C.
King David: Jerusalem as Israel's Capital   c.1000-961 B.C.
King Solomon: Golden Era – The First Temple Built   c.961-922 B.C.
Fall of Northern Kingdom of Israel   c. 722 B.C.
Fall of Jerusalem – Southern Kingdom of Judah   c. 586 B.C.

PERSIAN PERIOD   538-333 B.C.
The Return from Exile   538 B.C.
The Dedication of the Second Temple   c. 520-515 B.C.
Nehemiah Rebuilds Jerusalem's Walls   445 B.C.

HELLENISTIC PERIOD   c. 331-168 B.C.
Alexander the Great in Palestine   c. 331 B.C.
Maccabean Revolt   c. 168 B.C.

HASMONEAN PERIOD   c. 168-37 B.C.

ROMAN PERIOD   c. 37 B.C.-395 A.D.
King Herod the Great   c. 37 B.C.-4 A.D.
Crucifixion of Jesus   c. 29 A.D.
The Jews Revolt Against Rome   66-70 A.D.
Romans Destroy the Temple of Jerusalem   70 A.D.
Romans Capture Masada, the Last Stronghold   73 A.D.
Saint Helena Visits the Holy Land   326 A.D.

BYZANTINE RULE (CHRISTIANS)   395-638 A.D.
Persian Conquest of Palestine   614 A.D.
Heraclius Recaptures Palestine for Byzantines   628 A.D.

ARAB-MUSLIM RULE   638-1099 A.D.
Mohammed's Flight to Medina *(Hijira)*   622 A.D.
Caliph Omar Captures Jerusalem   638 A.D.
Dome of the Rock is Completed   691 A.D.
Seljuk Turks Replace Egyptians as Rulers of Jerusalem   1077 A.D.
First Crusade: Godfrey of Bouillon Takes Jerusalem   1099 A.D.

THE CRUSADERS' KINGDOM   1099-1291
Saladin Expels Crusaders   1187
The Third to the Eighth Crusades   1188-1250
The Fall of Acre: The End of Christian Rule   1291

THE MAMELUKES OF EGYPT RULE   1247-1517

THE OTTOMAN TURKS RULE   1517-1917
Selim I Occupies Jerusalem, Inaugurating Four Hundred Years of Turkish Rule   1517
Suleiman the Magnificent Rebuilds the City Walls   1540
Jerusalem is Governed by Mohammed Ali of Egypt and His Son Ibrahim   1832-1840
Palestine Restored to Turks   1841
Latin Patriarchate of Jerusalem Restored   1847
Anglican Bishopric Founded   1849

THE BRITISH MANDATE   1917-1948
General E. H. Allenby Takes Jerusalem   1917
Termination of British Mandate   May 14, 1948
The State of Israel Proclaims Independence   May 14, 1948

Foreword

This book represents a personal obligation, the repayment of a debt I owe the Holy Land. For I have lived this book. I lived it in Jerusalem, and from there it sent me forth, north to Dan, south to Beersheba, and beyond.

This book began to grow in me in December, 1967. As a pilgrim-resident spending a sabbatical year with my wife and daughters in the Holy City, I heard cannons heralding Islam's sacred month of Ramadan booming out at the very hours that I saw Christian pilgrims moving toward Bethlehem at Christmastime. And all the while, that very week, from our Jerusalem apartment I could see the dancing lights of myriads of Hanukkah menorahs across the city. The celebration of these three sacred seasons at one and the same time is an infrequent occurence.

And it was a time not long after a war — the war of June, 1967 — and the hope for peace, light, and human joy seemed distant indeed. Yet there, in and around Jerusalem, the three great religions still prayed and sang and dreamed of joy, and light, and peace. And they did so at sacred sites they had lovingly preserved and often shared. They did so, to be sure, in their own unmatched ways, yet their spiritual sagas are interrelated and connected as are few other human or divine stories. Indeed, it is in the Holy Land, as nowhere else on earth, that their epic stories are still visible, tangible, and self-revealing.

This personal experience in Jerusalem led me to seek out brothers-in-spirit all over the land. In the course of these encounters with people and places I came to know and to love the land in new ways: I saw it as the pre-eminent teacher for all who would pierce the mystery of the survival of spiritual traditions. So, to all men of good faith, and of every faith, I offer this historical guide to treasures they share — holy treasures of the land that have influenced the course of human civilization. Hopefully, for those who have already made their pilgrimage to the Holy Land, this book can serve as a lasting spiritual and historical memento. And for those who hope some day to go up to the land, it may help bring them there with deepened feelings and greater insights.

While I must obviously assume responsibility for all that appears here, it is a pleasant duty to record my sincere indebtedness to the men of Jerusalem of all the great religions who also introduced me to some of the hidden and invisible tales behind history — the personal and human sides to the historical sites and sacred places. Among Christians they include Bishop Shahe Ajamian of the Armenian Cathedral of St. James; Greek Orthodox Patriarch Benedictos and his colleagues; Father Elyakim, Greek Orthodox Priest-in-Charge of the Monastery of the Cross; the late Latin Patriarch, the Most Reverend Alberto Gori, and the office of the Franciscan Custos of the Holy Land; Father Bruno Hussar, Dominican head of the House of Isaiah, and members of his interesting community; Father Elpidius Pax, Director of the Franciscan Centre of Biblical Studies on the Via Dolorosa; Father Jean Roger, the Assumptionist Priest of Jerusalem's Notre Dame; the Reverend Peter Schneider, then adviser to the Anglican Archbishop of Jerusalem; Father Joseph

Stiasny, head of the Catholic Ratisbonne Centre; the Sisters of Sion of the Ecce Homo Church on the Via Dolorosa; Abbysinian, Coptic, and Russian Orthodox priests; and the Reverend Johan Snock of the Church of Scotland in Tiberias, a frequent companion in Jerusalem, and now Secretary of the Committee on the Church and the Jewish People, of the World Council of Churches, in Geneva, Switzerland.

I enjoyed the hospitality and had the benefit of several in-depth discussions with Aref al-Aref, widely regarded as "one of the most romantic Arab Muslims," at his al-Tireh home near Ramallah. A native of Jerusalem, formerly its Mayor, and a renowned advocate of the Arab cause, Aref al-Aref is also an expert on Jerusalem and the author of several histories. He is, above all, a recognized authority on Jerusalem's singular Dome of the Rock.

I cannot adequately express my gratitude to the many Jewish teachers, scholars, and librarians who were of help. I am, however, especially thankful to Dr. Jonah Malachy, expert on Jewish-Christian relations, of Israel's Ministry of Religions, and to his staff; and everlastingly to Dr. Zev Vilnay, Israel's foremost geographer-guide, with whom I walked almost every inch of historic Jerusalem and studied many other ancient sites in various parts of the country.

The Library of the Hebrew Union College School of Archaeology was most hospitable. Many of the pages that follow were first penned in that quiet and serene setting overlooking the walls of the Old City of Jerusalem.

In August, 1970, while in Israel, I assembled the photographs that will be found here. I record my thanks to David Appel, formerly of Toronto and now of Tivon, Israel, for his intelligent assistance and friendly counsel in this pleasant task.

As so often before, I have been aided and encouraged by untold kindnesses conferred upon me by my secretary, Rose Kushner, who helped prepare the manuscript for the press.

On Hanukkah, 5731, which coincides with Christmas, 1970, I conclude these lines in Toronto, miles removed from the Holy Land. But the light of that land shines everywhere. It reminds us that despite the cherished differences of the world's great religions, if God is to be their father, they must first be his children, and so become brothers.

S.E.R.
Toronto, Canada
December 25, 1970

Introduction: The Ancient Land

There are many holy books, a variety of holy bibles, a dazzling assortment of holy days and ways, and diverse holy men and places stretching across the earth's four corners. But there is only one Holy Land.

Judaism, Christianity, and Islam – the three major faiths that have most shaped world thought and human behaviour – are related to each other through their common origins in that land. Throughout their histories, the memory of those earliest beginnings has been kept alive, and thus the religions have maintained their spiritual connections with each other.

Monotheism, in other words, is not merely an idea in the minds of men; it is an idea with a concrete history in a specific place. And that history emerged in the life of those who were Semites: not physically but spiritually, for to borrow a phrase from Pope Pius XI, spiritually all monotheists are Semites. Clearly, all those who are "spiritual Semites" – Jews, Christians, and Muslims – share a holy history rooted in common experiences and traditions deriving from the Holy Land.

For each group, the Holy Land is something different. Yet for each it remains one and the same: an eternal centre for the evocation of older sanctities that still illumine the world.

The Holy Land is a land bridge between Africa, Asia, and Europe, and thus it has been and still remains a meeting place and combustion point of competing and disparate cultures, of rival empires, cults, and tongues. Its topography reveals its paradoxes. The land lies where the temperate zone meets the semi-tropical, and as a result sharp clefts rupture the crust of its earth, dividing this already tiny land into several distinctively different and apposite sub-regions. Judaca with its mountains, its rounded hills and deep-cut rocky valleys – so different from the more open Samaria; the southern Negev desert, so vastly dissimilar from the plains and mountain ridges of Galilee; the coastal plain, with its undulating lowlands, so unlike the isolated majesty of Jerusalem sitting enthroned atop the country's central heights.

Essential to the history and faith of Israel is the land of Israel. But geography, as everyone knows, helps fashion history, and history helps shape philosophical and theological concepts of man and God. What is the geography like? Palestine has narrow frontiers and numerous deserts; open and empty spaces visible from mountain tops that look out, east and west, upon salty seas; high places that quickly trickle down to the earth's lowest and hottest flat-lands; blue blazing skies and rocky wastes leading to arid dunes and flinty canyons; rapid and sudden changes in horizon and landscape; lush vineyards and fertile valleys, but also track after track of unwatered, unremembered land; hostile neighbours to the north and south, and empires ominously spreading about from every side. Palestine has a little of every country of the world.

All of these helped to make its flight to God Israel's primary salvation from ruin and extinction. "The Lord is my shepherd," the Psalmist could sing in the midst of every adversity, "I shall not want." (Psalm 23:1)

"By dread deeds thou dost answer us with deliverance, O God of our salvation ... who by thy strength hast established the mountains ... who dost still the roaring of the seas, the roaring of their waves, the tumult of peoples; so that those who dwell at earth's farthest bounds are afraid at thy signs. ..."
(Psalm 65:5-8)

The unique characteristics of the land which placed its stamp upon the Hebrew character and the Jewish religion have also left their indelible mark upon Christianity. The imprint of the land of Israel is everywhere to be found in the life and work of Jesus.

Unlike Judaism and Christianity, the roots of Islam flowered principally in the desert of Arabia, not in Palestine. But Islam has not forgotten its roots in the Holy Land. Abraham, father of the Jewish people, is also a Muslim venerable. He is *al-Khalil*, "the Friend," the Friend of God. And others of his family, those whom Jews know as their Patriarchs, share similar spiritual honours. Little wonder, then, that the land to which Abraham had come at the command of his God also became a part of Muslim spiritual history. Indeed, unwittingly, in helping to preserve the memory of these ancient ancestors in the very land of their earlier habitation, Islam kept alive the record of early Judaism in the land from which most Jews had been exiled. Sacred places to the history of the Old Testament were thus safeguarded and remembered by generations of Muslims who never ceased to venerate the memory of ancient Jewish biblical figures.

One has only to visit the Holy Land or study its terrain and holy places for visual signs of that common rootedness to come alive. The visitor or reader may trace the unending interconnections down through history which the three Great Faiths have shared in the land. Nowhere else save there, in the Holy Land, can one recognize, so simply and quickly, that the differences separating Judaism from Christianity, and each from Islam, are intimately related to their common background. They grew up as "members of the same family," in the same home, and as part of the same environment.

The Promised Land of Judaism became something else to Christians. For Jews, the unique relationship of the land of Israel to the religion of Israel serves as a sign and a vehicle of God's unending covenant with his people. For Christians, Palestine is the land of Messianic Promise; it brought forth the person of Jesus as Messiah and Saviour. His birth, life, and death on that soil hallow that land forever.

Thus the Land of Israel for Jews becomes the Land of Jesus, for Christians. The land of one nation becomes every man's land: the Zion of all nations. These are views that diverge and separate, and in the course of history often may even contradict each other. But all lead to the inevitable conclusion: Apart from the Holy Land, where Israel was born and nurtured, Judaism cannot be fully understood; nor can the life and teachings of Jesus be fully apprehended without knowing something of his land and his home. For his life work was not only *in*, but also *for*, that land. His ministry was within Palestine, the land he practically never left throughout his many journeys. And his speech is so impregnated with the style of Palestinian life that the rhythms, meters, and alliterations of Hebrew poetry can even be felt in the Greek of the Gospels.

Perhaps the most important reminders of the eternal and universal significance of the Holy Land to the life of the spirit everywhere are the Two Testaments, the Old and the New, sacred to Christians and Jews. Indeed, it was the Holy Bible which recorded for all time the life, times, fears, and hopes of the land and its peoples. And because of their possession of the Bible, or "the Book," as Muslims called it, Islam did not regard Jews and Christians as pagans or idolators against whom it should wage relentless war. They were "the People of the Book" who worshipped God, even if from the Muslim point of view in an imperfect manner.

Thus Jewish and Christian history came to be considered part of Muslim life and thought. Inevitably, the Land of Israel and the Land of Jesus also became a place of special significance to the followers of Mohammed.

The story of the Holy Land in the religious history of the world begins with Abraham – "friend of God" – who made a pact with the Lord. That pact, or *b'rith*, would be renewed later in his people's history, at Sinai, by Moses their teacher. That covenant explains why the Old Testament endured, and why later the New Testament would endure too. Virtually alone among the literatures of the ancient world, the Book survived the silt of time's deluge. From antiquity, it emerged as a unique and protected record of the earliest days of human history.

In the face of man's normal forgetfulness of his past, how could this miracle of history have occurred? The scholars of ancient Israel who were responsible for the authoring and editing of Scripture believed that what they wrote or gathered together derived from the one true God who entered into a unique covenant with his people, Israel. Those who sheltered and protected this literature as a living Scripture kept it as a holy book, preserved its language as a holy language, regarded the land of its birth as the Holy Land, called its significant sites holy places, and understood the events it records as universal because they constituted a sacred and redemptive history. This explains why it has come down to our day, if not completely intact, then surely as the most comprehensive summary of the culture of a people on its land ever to be safeguarded by so few, for so many, for so long.

Part One: In Bible Times
The Old Testament

THE PROMISED LAND

"Now the Lord said to Abram, 'Go from your country and your kindred and your father's house to the land that I will show you. And I will make of you a great nation, and I will bless you, and make your name great, so that you will be a blessing.' " (Genesis 12:1-2) Abram accepted the command, and with his acceptance the foundation was laid for the perpetual covenant between God and man. This, too, served as the continuing basis of the other religions that would flow forth from this land "shown to Abram" – the Promised Land.

"And Abram took Sarai his wife, and Lot his brother's son, and all their possessions which they had gathered . . . and they set forth to go to the land of Canaan. When they had come to the land of Canaan, Abram passed through the land to the place at Shechem, to the oak of Moreh. At that time the Canaanites were in the land. Then the Lord appeared to Abram, and said, 'To your descendants I will give this land.' So he built there an altar to the Lord, who had appeared to him." (Genesis 12:5-7)

Between Mount Gerizim and Mount Ebal, Abraham pitched his tent. It was there, at the entrance to this lovely valley, that the Lord appeared to him and offered him this promise of the future.

At this very place, generations later, Joshua entered the land of Canaan, at the head of the twelve tribes of Israel returning from Egypt, and in this beautiful valley, "made a covenant with the people that day, and made statutes and ordinances for them at Shechem." (Joshua 24:25) Shechem would become identified, thereafter, as the capital of the northern Kingdom of Israel, and, as such, it often stood in opposition to Jerusalem, capital of the southern Kingdom of Judah. Still later, when the Jews returned from their captivity in Babylon, they refused to consider those who had continued to inhabit Shechem and the surrounding area of Samaria as loyal and untainted Jews. These people became known as Samaritans – they were considered to be the descendants of Assyrian colonists who had intermarried with remnants of those Israelites who had not been deported earlier. They practised a syncretistic religion, an admixture of the Mosaic law interlaced with pagan practices.

These Samaritans were denied the privilege of helping in the rebuilding of the Temple in Jerusalem. This goaded them into complete and implacable separation from the Jews, and their hostility led them to establish a rival temple to the one in Jerusalem, atop Mount Gerizim.

Jesus, it is true, showed friendship toward them, yet this did not prevent Samaritans from offering Christians the same hostility they felt toward Jews. In our day, a scant four hundred Samaritans survive, most of whom live in the city of Nablus, Arabic for Neopolis, by which name the Romans came to call Shechem. At their picturesque ceremonies atop Mount Gerizim at Passover time, they slaughter twelve lambs, one for each tribe of Israel, as a Paschal sacrifice. It is then that we call to mind the ancient assembly of Israel's tribes in the valley between Ebal and Gerizim. All of this, because of Abraham – Abraham, the friend of God, who first received the promise of the land, at that valley in Shechem where "there builded he an altar unto the Lord."

From Shechem at a time of famine, Abraham went down into Egypt to sojourn. When he left Egypt, he went by stages to Beth-El, where he separated from his nephew Lot, for their herds and retinue were becoming too numerous. "Then Abram said to Lot, 'Let there be no strife between you and me . . . is not the whole land before you?' " (Genesis 13: 8-9) Given first choice, Lot decided on the rich-looking Jordan Valley, and followed it down to Sodom, south of the Dead Sea, which in earlier days was known as the Sea of Salt.

Practically desolate, the area of the Dead Sea is an appropriate setting for the enactment of the Biblical drama of human sin and divine judgment. Abraham endeavoured to intercede before the Lord on behalf of the erring human communities of Sodom and Gomorrah. Pleading their cause he dared challenge God:

"Far be it from thee to do such a thing, to slay the righteous with the wicked . . . shall not the Judge of all the earth do right?" (Genesis 18:25) But not even a handful of righteous men could be found. "Then the Lord rained on Sodom and Gomorrah brimstone and fire from the Lord out of heaven; and he overthrew those cities, and all the valley and all the inhabitants of the cities, and what grew on the ground. But Lot's wife behind him looked back, and she became a pillar of salt." (Genesis 19: 24-26)

Coming down to the Dead Sea at Sodom, the world's lowest level, one needs no further elaboration of the sense of desolation and the feeling of total disconnection with the rest of the land – indeed, with reality itself. "Lo, the smoke of the land went up like the smoke of a furnace." The sea forms an unusual soft and smooth blue base to the harsh deserts surrounding – Scripture's description abides. The rocky white earth is dry and barren; in the distance pale and dark mountains give off mists that resemble smoky columns – the land appears cursed for the sins of men who do not hearken. Other cities in history have been decried as Sodoms too, but only this "city" remains.

After Lot had separated from him, the Lord appeared unto Abram and said: " 'Lift up your eyes, and look from the place where you are, northward and southward and eastward and westward; for all the land which you see I will give to you and to your descendants for ever . . . Arise, walk through the length and the breadth of the land, for I will give it to you.' So Abram moved his tent, and came and dwelt by the oaks of Mamre, which are at Hebron; and there he built an altar to the Lord." (Genesis 13: 14-18)

HEBRON AND THE PATRIARCHS

Hebron is one of the oldest towns in the East. According to the Old Testament it was founded seven years before Zoan, the capital of Lower Egypt, known as Tanis, making it close to 3,700 years old.

Positioned on four hills, the Bible also refers to Hebron as *Kiryat-Arba*, the "town of four." It is situated at one of the greatest heights in all of the Holy Land, some 927 meters above sea level. Abraham's grove of terebinths, or oaks, became his first real home since setting out on his long wanderings from Ur of the Chaldees to Canaan, thence to Egypt, until he returned finally to the land promised him.

The tradition that Hebron was his first place of establishment in the land is what has made this city one of four sacred to Jews — the others being Jerusalem, Tiberias and Safad. But since Abraham and his son Ishmael are believed by Muslims to have built their most sacred shrine, the Ka'aba in Mecca, Hebron, as Abraham's encampment, has also become a city of special significance to Muslims. The Koran, their Sacred Book, says: "Allah [the Almighty] adopted Abraham as a friend." Thus for almost a thousand years Arabs have called Hebron *al-Khalil*, as a constant reminder of "Allah's friend."

Friend of God, and favoured by him, Abraham was approaching advanced age, still lacking what he must have very dearly wanted – a son, to give meaning to the covenant, through whom he could hand down the tradition. Sara, his wife, gave him her maid Hagar as a concubine, and she bore him a son, Ishmael. "He shall be a wild ass of a man, his hand against every man and every man's hand against him." (Genesis 16:12)

Ishmael, apparently the first of the Bedouins, is precious to Muslims in a way he is not to Jews. For the latter, Isaac, the father of Jacob, and thus grandfather of the children of Israel (as Jacob was also known), is the spiritual heir of Abraham. Abraham, apparently, had migrated often into the Negev area, westward across the Hebron hills. At the edge of the wilderness, in the northern Negev, he dug a well and planted a tamarisk tree, and there called upon the name of the Lord. There, too, in what came to be known as Beersheba, Isaac was probably born to Sara, in Abraham's hundredth year!

It was somewhere in the Negev, perhaps indeed at Beersheba, that Abraham, God's friend, was put to the supreme test, emerging ultimately, in Soren Kierkegaard's telling phrase, as "The Knight of Faith." Indeed, the Old Testament story of the binding of Isaac, forms the basis of profound theological developments across the years within Christianity as much as in Judaism. The fundamental biblical idea of the call to sacrifice the beloved son to God, for the sake of God, has been incorporated into many Christian theologies.

Possibly, then, from Beersheba towards Moriah, Abraham set out that fateful morning. "Take your son, your only son Isaac, whom you love, and go to the land of Moriah, and offer him there as a burnt-offering upon one of the mountains of which I shall tell you." (Genesis 22:2) Abraham did not hesitate. He saddled a donkey, took two servants, split some wood, and with his son Isaac set out for the destination. For three days they travelled to "the place of which God had told him."

No words were spoken throughout the three excruciatingly painful days of the journey. "Then on the third day Abraham lifted up his eyes, and saw the place afar off." The place cannot be pinpointed since nothing was ever set aside to mark it off. But Jewish, Christian, and Muslim traditions are all certain of the location: precisely on Mount Moriah, in the old city of Jerusalem, the exact place where Solomon had built his temple, the site of the Holy of Holies. Still later, this was the place of Herod's Temple, frequently visited by Jesus and his disciples. And later still, from this very place, on this very rock, Muslims believe that Mohammed ascended to heaven on the wings of an angel in the form of a magical steed, *al-Buraq*, after a night's ride from Mecca to Jerusalem. Their unusual shrine, the Dome of the Rock, has been built at this very place, and it magnificently shelters this self-same rock, the altar-stone of Isaac's near sacrifice.

Not long after this harrowing but elevating experience atop Moriah, Abraham returned to his place in Hebron. "Sarah died . . . and Abraham went in to mourn for Sarah and to weep for her." (Genesis 23:2) Long a wanderer, the time had now come for Abraham to link himself to a particular place: He needed to bury his dead. The sojourner had at last become a permanent resident, for the dead require a permanent place to abide. "And Abraham rose up from before his dead, and said to the Hittites, 'I am a stranger and a sojourner among you; give me property among you for a burying place, that I may bury my dead out of my sight.' " (Genesis 23: 3-4) For four hundred shekels of silver, Ephron the Hittite sold him his field, "in Machpelah, which was to the east of Mamre, the field with the cave which was in it and all the trees that were in the field." (Genesis 23:17)

In the course of time, Abraham was also laid to rest in the Cave of Machpelah, for he "was old, well advanced in years; and the Lord had blessed Abraham in all things." (Genesis 24:1) Subsequently, the remains of the other two Jewish Patriarchs, Isaac and Jacob, and their wives Rebekah and Leah, were also placed in the Cave. Today, in Hebron, one can visit Machpelah, known since Muslim times as *al-Haram al-Ibrahim*. The "Sanctuary of Abraham" serves as a mosque. Much of the present edifice dates back to the Middle Ages, following the Muslim conquest of Palestine. But the lower portions of the enclosing walls are unmistakably from the period of Herod the Great, and probably date back to a time within a few years before the birth of Jesus. They are still in a remarkable state of good repair.

Christians, in Byzantine times, used to make pilgrimages to this site of the patriarchal sepulchre, and eventually a church was erected within the area for the benefit of these pious pilgrims. But when Caliph Omar conquered Palestine, the sacred relics of beloved Abraham could not fail to interest Muslims, and the sepulchre was transformed into a mosque. When Hebron was captured by the Crusaders in the twelfth century, the Haram and its annexes were turned into a Castle Garrison quarter and a monastery, and the older Byzantine church was restored. After the Crusades, the mosque was rebuilt, and strict regulations preventing non-Muslims from entering the enclosure were vigorously enforced. Indeed, until 1967, Jews who wished to come near the Tombs to pray could only go as far as the fifth step on the northern staircase, and only from there could offer up their petitions, in the name of "the God of Abraham, Isaac and Jacob." Today, the Machpelah is still a mosque for Muslim prayer and study, but people of all faiths may now enter freely, and at the patriarchal cenotaphs themselves, Jewish worship services are now conducted thrice daily.

RACHEL'S TOMB

While Jacob is entombed in the family sepulchre at Hebron, his beloved wife Rachel, who died while giving birth to Benjamin, is buried near Bethlehem. "So Rachel died, and she was buried on the way to Ephrath [that is,Bethlehem], and Jacob set up a pillar upon her grave; it is the pillar of Rachel's tomb, which is

there to this day." (Genesis 35:19-20) Rachel, in later biblical tradition, plays the role of the weeping mother of hurt and exiled children who pass by her grave on the road to Bethlehem.

"Why did Jacob bury Rachel on the way to Bethlehem?" the rabbis of the Talmud inquired. And they answered, "Jacob foresaw that the exiled children of Israel would pass that way, so he buried her there that she might ask mercy for them." And similarly, St. Matthew, when describing Herod's slaughter of Bethlehem's innocent children, reverts to the image of a weeping Rachel to represent the grief of the mothers of Bethlehem bereft of their babies. In doing so, Matthew recalls Jeremiah's prophecy which had pictured Rachel bewailing the fate of her children as they departed to their exile. "A voice was heard in Ramah, wailing and loud lamentation, Rachel weeping for her children; she refused to be consoled, because they were no more." (Matthew 2:18, quoting Jeremiah 31:15)

Rachel's tomb, thus, has a special significance to Jews, Christians, and Muslims. The Crusaders rebuilt the sepulchre during their days in the Holy Land. Later, Muslims began to venerate the tomb, and even prohibited Christians from entering it, so sacred did they consider the place to be. In 1841, Sir Moses Montefiore, the British Jewish leader, obtained the keys for the Jews to *Qubbet Rahil*, Rachel's Tomb, and with the exception of the period of Jordanian rule (from 1948 to 1967), Jews have since been in the habit of making pilgrimages there. Indeed, of the ten holy places officially recognized as those of the three faiths, Rachel's Tomb, near Bethlehem, together with the Western or Wailing Wall of the Jerusalem Temple, have been internationally regarded as "Jewish Holy Places."

JACOB'S WELL AND JOSEPH'S TOMB

Jacob and Rachel lie buried in Judah, and the family tomb too is situated in Hebron. In later days Hebron also served as David's capital for more than seven years, before he went up to Jerusalem. But the northern tribeland of Ephraim is not without important historical remembrances as well. The role of Shechem has been noted. It is now appropriate to discuss two additional sites in that northern Israelite stronghold which not only bear reminiscences of the Hebrew Patriarchs but have also wielded continuing and interconnecting influences upon the Christian, the Muslim, and even the Samaritan traditions.

When Jacob returned home from his sojourn with Laban in Mesopotamia, and with his family and flocks "came safely to the city of Shechem, which is in the land of Canaan . . . and he camped before the city . . . he bought for a hundred pieces of money the piece of land on which he had pitched his tent. There he erected an altar and called it El-Elohe-Israel." (Genesis 33: 18-20)

There, in Jacob's fields, the well which he dug for himself, his children, and his cattle, has been preserved over the centuries, and as early as 404, in the time of St. Jerome, mention is made of a Christian church in these fields of Jacob, with the historic well in the centre of its crypt. St. John recorded a moving description of Jesus' encounter with the Samaritan woman who had come to draw water from this very well. It was essentially in recollection of this scriptural event that Christians have preserved Jacob's Well in the sacred setting of a church.

Close to Jacob's Well is Joseph's Tomb. Moses had brought the remains of Joseph from Egypt. "And Moses took the bones of Joseph with him; for Joseph had solemnly sworn the people of Israel, saying, 'God will visit you; then you must carry my bones with you from here.' " (Exodus 13:19) Moses never did reach the Promised Land. But his faithful follower, Joshua, did, and he saw to it that Joseph's urgent testament was carried out. "The bones of Joseph which the people of Israel brought up from Egypt were buried at Shechem, in the portion of ground which Jacob bought from the sons of Hamor . . . it became an inheritance of the descendants of Joseph." (Joshua 24:32) Indeed, the tomb, known in Arabic as *Qabr Yusif*, has two pillars on either side of the entrance. According to the Muslim tradition which helped to preserve this site, both pillars served as memorials to Joseph's children, Ephraim and Manasseh. This white-domed building, built like an Arabic *weli*, has also retained its spiritual interest for Christians. St. Paul's Epistle to the Hebrews, which gives as examples of faith "the assurance of things hoped for, the conviction of things not seen," considers Joseph's testament concerning his burial in the land of the Fathers an example of faith – his faith in the promise of the Promised Land.

MOSES IN SINAI

History, it has been said, was born on that night when Moses led his people forth from Goshen, in the land of Egypt.

To this day, throughout the Sinai Peninsula, from north to south, the name and the story of Moses predominate. The highest peak in the central part of the Sinai range is called after him – the name given to it by revering Arabs is *Jebel Musa*, or Mount Moses. For some 1,500 years Bedouins have been pointing to this peak as the Biblical Mount Sinai, the place of God's revelation to the children of Israel, after their exodus from Egypt. And the stone at Horeb they have been calling the "Rock of Moses" because they identify it as the very rock the Lord told Moses to smite, in answer to the people's complaints of dire thirst – "And water shall come out of it, that the people may drink." (Exodus 17:6)

Sinai belongs to Moses. And through Moses and his people it has come into the heritage of Christianity and Islam. The dramatic tales of his ancient wanderings and achievements in this desolate wilderness have become a principal source of inspiration in all of the three great religions. Of all places in the world, Sinai does indeed seem most suited to its purpose and its mission: that awesome and isolated region where, amid "the thunderings and the lightnings and the sound of the trumpet and the mountain smoking," the commandments of the Lord were given to Israel and the world.

To the Israelites coming up to the land of Canaan from Egypt, the arid "Alps of Arabia" planted in the desert must have seemed eerie and strange in contrast to the green valleys of the Nile they had left after their Egyptian bondage. They were now enclosed within a sanctuary of temples and pyramids made not by human hands. Sinai is a fiercely natural outdoor prison, isolated and separated from the great world beyond. Only occasionally did they reach springs, wells, and brooks – places like the waters of Marah, the springs of Elim, the brook of Horeb, and the well of Jethro in Midian.

These experiences of the Israelites in Sinai formed the foreground and remained an important basis for their future religious orientation. The harsh and rugged life of the desert gave birth to a religion which called for co-operative human effort, just dealings, equality before the law, and the need to create a human community that would incarnate God's word and teaching within the social order. All of these significant hopes grew out of the desert experience, and the inescapable burden which a lonely and pensive isolation places upon human conscience to hearken to the law of God speaking out of the whirlwind. In the desert all men are equal. In the desert one God is the father of all who are, necessarily, brothers.

As early as the beginning of the fourth century it is believed that a tower had been built by Christians in Sinai, at a site thought to be the place where, according to desert traditions, the divine voice had spoken to Moses out of the bush that "was burning, yet it was not consumed." The Roman Emperor Justinian some years later built a fortified convent at the same place. It had massive walls and was called the Great Convent of Transfiguration. The remains of the martyred Saint Catherine of Alexandria were later transferred to this place atop Mount Sinai, and thereafter it took on her name, becoming the Monastery of St. Catherine. In those pre-Islamic centuries, camping near the palm groves of Firan, and the springs of Jebel Musa, were probably no less than six thousand monks and hermits; many were originally pilgrims from Armenia and Syria who had remained in the Holy Land. Of all the cells and small convents which have housed them, only the massive, fortress-like St. Catherine Monastery has endured the assault of time.

This convent, ironically, has probably remained as the one seat of Christian worship in all of Arabia. Indeed, atop the same mountain, and within the walls of the convent, there is also a mosque. The Greek Orthodox monks of St. Catherine's, the only priests in the midst of a Muslim sea, have wisely allowed Muslims to pray side by side with Christian pilgrims.

The old Muslim tradition, which cannot be proved or disproved yet is staunchly maintained, is that Mohammed, while still a camel-driver in Arabia, wandered by and spent time at this very place, when the convent was about a century old. Indeed, the Koran makes repeated references to the stone of Moses. First Moses was said to have reposed on it; later Mohammed too. In the Middle Ages, Christian pilgrims also venerated the stone, and they carved crosses in the rock as a sign of homage and a mark of their piety.

Moses, then, remains the great central figure of the Sinai desert. He is remembered by Jews, for whom he is their masterful rabbi-teacher; by Christian pilgrims, who come to the place where the Lord spoke to him and to the children of Israel; and by Muslims, for whom he is a saintly prophet, the venerated *Nebi Musa*. But he never reached the land himself.

"And Moses went up from the plains of Moab to Mount Nebo, to the top of Pisgah, which is opposite Jericho. And the Lord showed him all the land, Gilead as far as Dan, all Naphtali, the land of Ephraim and Manasseh, all the land of Judah as far as the Western Sea, the Negeb, and the Plain, that is, the valley of Jericho the city of palm trees, as far as Zoar. And the Lord said to him, 'This is the land of which I swore to Abraham, to Isaac, and to Jacob, "I will give it to your descendants." I have let you see it with your eyes, but you shall not go over there.' So Moses the servant of the Lord died there in the land of Moab. . . ." (Deuteronomy 34:1-5)

JERICHO

Jericho, perhaps the world's most ancient city, is at least ten thousand years old. Late in the thirteenth century B.C., when the Israelites, under Joshua, crossed over the Jordan to conquer Jericho and proceeded to settle Canaan, the city had already known many battles, sieges, and destructions. Always important because of its abundant sources of water, Jericho, which the Bible calls "the city of palm trees," is a beautiful oasis rising on hundreds of springs. It luxuriates in green, in the very middle of harsh, wild and stark desert lands. Nearby are the rocky, barren cliffs of the Judaean wilderness, dropping abruptly to the northern perimeter of the Dead Sea. Made part of their tribal patrimony, it fell to the lot of the men of Benjamin to defend Jericho from the constant threat of outside attack.

In the days of the Judges, Eglon, King of Moab, conquered "the city of palm trees" and "the people of Israel served Eglon the king of Moab eighteen years." (Judges 3:14) But at last Moab was subdued: Ehud, the left-handed Benjaminite, smote the King, and from the hill country went down to Jericho and then to the fords of the Jordan, against the Moabites. "And the land had rest for eighty years." (Judges 3:30)

Doubtless because of its unique location and topography – its proximity to mountains, a river, a desert, and a sulphuric sea – in later biblical years Jericho became the scene of important spiritual events. There, the "sons of the prophets" had dwelled and meditated, and probably lived together as members of a prophetic school. There, at the banks of the Jordan, Elijah went up by a whirlwind to heaven. There, Elisha, took his mantle that had fallen, smote the waters, and they divided (II Kings 2). There, too, in a nearby mountain cave, Jesus underwent his fast of forty days, recollecting the forty years of Israelite wandering in the desert. "And he was in the wilderness forty days, tempted by Satan; and he was with the wild beasts; and the angels ministered to him." (Mark 1:13) Later still, on his way to Jerusalem, he entered and passed through Jericho.

For centuries thereafter, through the Byzantine period, Jews and Christians continued to live in Jericho, side by side, building their synagogues and churches in this lovely and historic town which sits quietly in the midst of the wilderness. Bodies of water, deserts, and mountains – these are the land's major contours that have placed their stamp on the spiritual history following its setttlement by Joshua. Places that had once been the scene of mighty battles in later memory were often transformed into remembrances of spiritual, not only military victories.

MOUNT TABOR

Majestic Mount Tabor, the frontier line of the northern tribes, was one such mountain site. Situated six miles due east of Nazareth, it rises nobly some 588 meters up from the surrounding valleys; it is set apart and can be distinguished from all sides for many miles. There Deborah, the prophetess and judge of Israel, had inspired Barak to defeat Sisera, the Canaanite military captain, with his chariots and multitudes.

Tabor, too, must have been one of the most favoured mountains for meditation and worship. Undoubtedly influenced by Canaanites, the Israelites had set up altars at its top and regarded it as a holy height. The Psalmist thought of it as an eternal and joyful witness, together with Mount Hermon, of the glory of the Lord. "Tabor and Hermon joyously praise thy name." (Psalms 89:12). "Tabor among the mountains" is how Jeremiah referred to this uniquely beautiful site. In the New Testament it is the "high mountain" that is the place of the Transfiguration. Nowhere in the Gospels is Tabor precisely mentioned but, according to all old traditions, it was indeed Tabor, "an high mountain" where this event took place:

"And he was transfigured before them, and his face shone like the sun, and his garments became white as light. And behold, there appeared to them Moses and Elijah ... and a voice from the cloud said, 'This is my beloved Son, with whom I am well pleased.' " (Matthew 17:2-5)

FIVE PHILISTINE CITIES

Various "sea peoples" from the Aegean had always been attacking the Egyptian imperial power, and in the twelfth century B.C., the Philistines, one of these maritime nations from afar, invaded the Egyptian colony of Canaan. The Pharaohs of the day were not strong enough to repel them, and they settled along the coastal plain, where they established five central cities – Gath, Gaza, Ekron, Ashdod, and Ashkelon. Archaeologists have demonstrated that when they came to Ashkelon they utterly destroyed the older Canaanite town, and built a new city, basing its life upon their own more developed material civilization.

It was but a few generations earlier that the Israelites had themselves entered the land from Transjordan to the east, settling in the country's interior. It is no surprise, therefore, to find the Bible repeatedly referring, during the period of the Judges following Joshua, to a series of clashes and conflicts between the two peoples, as the Philistines sought to penetrate from the coastal plain into the hinterland occupied by the Israelites.

Samson, perhaps more than anyone else in that period, tried to save Israel from the Philistine terror. When he was still a young man, "the spirit of the Lord came mightily upon him, and he went down to Ashkelon and killed thirty men of the town, and took their spoil." (Judges 14:19) The mighty Samson came to his own downfall in nearby Gaza when, as a Philistine prisoner, he destroyed three thousand of his enemies, as he tore down the pillars of the Temple of Dagon, crying, "Let me die with the Philistines." (Judges 16:30)

It remained for David, however, to destroy completely the Philistine hold upon the country. He followed Israel's first King, Saul, who had been the first to achieve any success in denting their lines. But alas, King Saul was to die doing battle with the Philistines at Mount Gilboa. Saul's army was poorly organized, in flight and disarray, his own sons killed, and he, himself, wounded. In an act of gallantry,

at Gilboa, he fell upon his sword to prevent his being taken alive:

"When the Philistines came to strip the slain, they found Saul and his three sons fallen on Mount Gilboa. And they cut off his head, and stripped off his armor, and sent messengers throughout the land of the Philistines to carry the good news to their idols . . . and they fastened his body to the wall of Beth-shan." (I Samuel 31:8-10) There follows, in the opening chapter of the Second Book of Samuel, David's moving lament over the tragic death of King Saul, and his own dearest companion, the King's son, Jonathan:

"Tell it not in Gath, publish it not in the streets of Ashkelon; lest the daughters of the Philistines rejoice . . . ye mountains of Gilboa, let there be no dew or rain upon you . . . for there the shield of the mighty was defiled . . . how are the mighty fallen in the midst of the battle!" (II Samuel 1:20-25)

This was a fateful hour in the history of Israel. Few biblical figures, or other ancient heroes for that matter, have remained as vivid as King David – and few as beloved, even in his hours of backsliding. Born in Bethlehem, in the tribeland of Judah, he came from the stock of an interesting union – of Ruth, the Moabite, and Boaz, kinsman of Naomi. David is the symbol, *par excellence*, of Jewish royalty. But even more, the House of David is the House of the Messiah.

At first, David reigned over Judah alone, at Hebron. After successfully ridding himself of his main rivals, and gaining the adherence of the northern tribes, he turned to his most urgent tasks: to remove from his people the yoke of Philistine domination, and to destroy the remaining pockets of Canaanite resistance which had survived the Israelite conquest. When he achieved these, he could look forward to his transcendent hope: to make Jerusalem the centre of a united country.

THE CITY OF DAVID

Until the time of David, the fortress town of Jerusalem was avoided by the leaders of Israel, and it remained the key hinge – still beyond them – between the northern and southern tribes. The Jebusites who dwelled in Jerusalem felt safe and secure behind its high and thick walls. They did not fear David. Indeed, they told him:

" 'You will not come in here, but the blind and the lame will ward you off' – thinking, 'David cannot come in here.' Nevertheless David took the stronghold of Zion, that is, the city of David. And David said on that day, 'Whoever would smite the Jebusites, let him get up the water shaft to attack the lame and the blind. . . .' " (II Samuel 5:6-8)

"And Joab the son of Zeruiah went up first, so he became chief." (I Chronicles 11:6) This is not only an insight into David's military strategy but also a significant clue to the extreme importance of water to the life and security of the mountain city of Jerusalem. Moreover, it provides an important landmark in helping to locate, fairly exactly, the site of the early Jerusalem of the Jebusites. It is on the eastern ridge, the Ophel, close by this ever-vital source of water. The "water-shaft" or water-pipe which Joab successfully climbed and captured was part of the ancient hydraulic installation drilled into the eastern hill of Ophel, and in many ways was similar to others built elsewhere – at Gezer, Gibeon, and Megiddo.

Water has always been the lifeline of Jerusalem and the land. Indeed, a reminder of this is the undeniable fact that various cisterns and wells, throughout the land, have been preserved as sacred sites. One can not always be certain that traditional sources actually coincide with the exact locations of these sites. For instance, at David's birthplace, Bethlehem, three great cisterns excavated in the rock have been called *Biyar Daud*, David's Wells, identifying them with "the well of Bethlehem which is by the gate." These were the waters for which David had longed during his battle with the Philistines. What is important is the role water played in the minds of those who lived in the Holy Land, and how ardently they have endeavoured to preserve what could not always be accurately preserved: the very place where ancient living waters still run.

After David's successful conquest of its water system, Jerusalem became the King's personal property. Thus it came to be called the City of David. But David wanted it to be more than his city; he wished for it to be the heart and soul of the whole country. And to accomplish this, he would have to make it the religious centre of the people. He would have to bring the Ark of the Covenant to the city. From Kiryat-Yearim, near the border of Benjamin and Judah, where Eleazar, son of Abinadab, was sanctified to keep the Ark of the Lord, he made arrangements for its festive and joyful arrival in the city. Kiryat-Yearim is also the Arab-Christian village of Abu-Ghosh, whose church is known as Our Lady of the Ark of the Covenant and which local Arabs have long known as *Dir-al-Azar*, Eleazar's Monastery, in affectionate remembrance of the one who had safeguarded the Ark before David brought it up to Jerusalem.

David never lived to build the great Temple to the glory of his God; that was left for his son, Solomon. But the Bible tells of his preparations: how he bought the threshing floor of Arauna, the Jebusite, westward of his city, and offered up sacrifices on the altar he had built there. Arauna's threshing floor, tradition holds, is the same summit of Mount Moriah where Abraham was believed to have brought Isaac for sacrifice. By associating the location of the sacrifice of Isaac with the great sanctuary of Jerusalem, the Biblical writers were indulging in a very natural tendency. They were interested in enhancing the prestige of Jerusalem as the sole authorized centre for Jewish worship, the only altar for the offering of sacrifices to the Lord.

It was this move from the Ophel, David's city, to Moriah, where Solomon was to build the Temple, that has caused some confusion to later generations. In the course of time, Moriah was identified with the Citadel of Zion. Later still, the original "City of David," which had been on the south side of Jerusalem's present-day walls, was moved westward in the popular mind, and it was believed to have

incorporated both a palace and a citadel. This explains why the Citadel, built by Herod almost a thousand years after the time of David, and situated in Herodian Jerusalem, came to be called the Tower of David to this day. It also explains why it happened that, after the fall of the Temple to the Romans in 70 A.D., once the Jewish Temple of Zion had passed away, the new "Christian" Zion arose south of what was erroneously called David's Tower. Indeed, what is now called Mount Zion is a different hill from the Zion of David's city, and is wrongly endowed with the identity of the original. The "Mount Zion" of today is clearly outside of the boundaries of both David's Ophel and Solomon's Temple on Moriah.

Based upon legends current among Christians after the fifth century, it was believed that the words of St. Peter that the "sepulchre of David is with us" meant that he was buried near the Cenacle on "Christian" Mount Zion. It was there that the Eucharist was instituted at the Last Supper in the Upper Room. Neither Jews nor Muslims had any certain traditions of the burial place of David, but in the course of time this Christian legend – that he was indeed buried at the site of the Cenacle – led Muslims to build a mosque at this place, and also to erect a huge cenotaph to the memory of David. "David's Tomb" on "Mount Zion" is still considered sacred to many. Nevertheless, the search for the real city of David and the real tomb of David goes on, conducted by learned archaeologists despite the popular acceptance of these other sites.

KING SOLOMON'S ACHIEVEMENTS

The great works which Solomon, his favourite son, carried out were originally planned by David. The peace which fortunately attended Solomon's reign allowed the youthful and wise monarch to embellish Jerusalem, his native and capital city, to establish and develop secure fortresses and water systems in various other parts of the country. He also expanded trade and commerce with countries to the north and south, and even across the seas from the southern Negev port of Elath. Indeed, Solomon had made "a fleet of ships . . . on the shore of the Red Sea." (I Kings 9:26)

The Fountain of Gihon in the Valley of Kidron was Jerusalem's principal spring, its major source of water. It was outside of the walls of the city and so presented a serious security problem since it could not be defended. It was thus necessary that the waters of the Gihon be connected to the city by means of underground engineering. The Jebusites had done just this, but once the "water shaft" was ingeniously taken by David's captain Joab, they were defeated and the city passed into the hands of David. In later days, different schemes were developed to help protect the city's water supply from falling into enemy hands, as it had in the days of the Jebusites.

Clearly, the Fountain of Gihon was one of Jerusalem's most important and crucial places, and the fact that David had chosen it as the site for the public anointing of Solomon as King, at the hands of Zadok the Priest, testifies to its very special prominence in the popular mind. In the days of the Temple, the waters of Gihon were taken in a golden can for the joyous libation held annually in the courts of the sanctuary on the Feast of Tabernacles. For Christians, too, the Gihon has become a place of historic reminiscence. There Mary drew water to wash Jesus' clothes, and since then it has also been called "The Fountain of the Virgin."

The foundations of the Temple of Jerusalem were laid during the fourth year of Solomon's reign, and work on the building continued for more than seven years, from about 957 to about 950 B.C. Solomon's name has been immortalized by the Temple which he built, and because of it he has entered the annals of history. But Solomon concerned himself not only with the peaceful activities of Temple-building but also with the need to fortify and secure his country from possible attack. In addition to the "wall of Jerusalem," he chose three strategic places in the country and made them into fortified cities – Hazor, Megiddo, and Gezer.

To finance these important structures he taxed the people with a special levy: "And this is the account of the forced labour which King Solomon levied to build the house of the Lord and his own house and the Millo and the wall of Jerusalem and Hazor and Megiddo and Gezer." (I Kings 9:15) (The "Millo" has been the subject of much speculation; no one is yet certain what it actually was. Kathleen Kenyon and other archaeologists believe the "Millo" was a series of stone-filled terraces which were important in defending the walls of Jerusalem from possible attack.)

Megiddo is situated strategically at the east-west crossing of Jezreel, and at the head of a mountain pass that guards access to the north from the coastal plain – along the important ancient trade and military route, *Via Maris*, the crucial trunk from Egypt in the south, to Syria and Mesopotamia in the north. Little wonder, then, that Solomon took such great pains to fortify and develop it as a major part of his national policy of peace and trade.

Megiddo is barely remembered today under that name, but most are familiar with Armageddon. Megiddo happens to be Armageddon, for the Greeks added "Ara" – the name of the nearby wadi – to "Megiddo." Its strategic location, as a point of possible contention between northern and southern empires, undoubtedly also led to its acquiring a very new and specific meaning in the Christian theological vocabulary. The Book of Revelation identified Megiddo (Armageddon) as the site of the ultimate earthly battle between the forces of good and evil. Indeed, Armageddon is regarded symbolically as the ongoing struggle between the righteous and unrighteous forces on earth.

The so-called "Solomon's Stables" in Jerusalem are also remembered today. The famous Basilica built by Emperor Justinian at the southeast corner of the Temple court, which served as a major centre for Christian pilgrims to the Holy Land, no longer stands. But when it was built, it had to be erected over mighty substructures, most of which were from the time of Herod, but others were ascribed to Solomon himself. Tradition suggested they were the understructures he had built for his horses. The Old Testament refers to a time when Queen Athalia was taken out of the Temple to be assassinated outside of its holy precincts: "And she went through the horses' entrance to the king's house." (II Kings 11:16) And Nehemiah, describing the various gates leading to the Temple Mount, mentions the "Horse Gate," at the southeast corner.

Still another of Solomon's achievements has endured. It has only recently come to life, but it is now functioning once again, thanks to an archaeologist's discovery. The Book of Deuteronomy described a country "whose stones are iron, and out of whose hills you can dig copper." (Deuter-onomy 8:9) Not long ago Dr. Nelson Glueck, an American archaeologist, revealed that Solomon had not only developed a navy in his port of Elath, as mentioned in the Bible, but actually used it as a merchant marine to transport the copper ingots produced in the huge smelters he had built at nearby Ezion-Geber. The Bible describes how his ships "went to Ophir, and brought from there gold, to the amount of four hundred and twenty talents; and they brought it to King Solomon." (I Kings 9:28) He apparently made use of copper as the medium of exchange, and with his successful industry, so near a natural port, he could bring back to his kingdom from the far East many precious goods.

The major mining site, which since Glueck's rediscovery has been put to use by the State of Israel, was at Timna. There, as if standing permanently on guard as dutiful sentries watching over Solomon's mines, are two huge rock-columns, which to this day are known as The Pillars of Solomon. Not only was Solomon a wise monarch, as countless legends regarded him, but he was a king who knew how to exploit the engineering and scientific knowledge of his day for the political and economic security of his country. So great was his reputation that certain advanced engineering feats, like those involved with the hydraulics of the so-called Solomon's Pools near Bethlehem, have been erroneously ascribed to him.

But the relatively peaceful days of Solomon did not outlast him. Internally, the kingdom was split into two, and the older antagonisms between the northern and southern tribes were brought into the open by a series of rebellions. In 722 B.C., the northern Kingdom of Israel fell; its people were conquered and taken into exile by the invading Assyrians.

ISAIAH – PROPHET OF PEACE

In the southern Kingdom of Judah, at
the capital city of Jerusalem, there lived
a prophet known as Isaiah in the days of
Kings Uzziah, Jotham, Ahaz, and
Hezekiah. He dreamed of internal peace:
"Ephraim shall not be jealous of Judah,
and Judah shall not harass Ephraim."
(Isaiah 11:13) But concerning Jerusalem
he also had a universal vision of its future
meaning to all peoples.

"It shall come to pass in the latter days that
the mountain of the house of the Lord
shall be established as the highest of the
mountains . . . and many peoples shall
come, and say, 'Come, let us go up to the
mountain of the Lord, to the house of
the God of Jacob; that he may teach us his
ways and that we may walk in his
paths.' For out of Zion shall go forth the
law, and the word of the Lord from
Jerusalem. He shall judge between the
nations, and shall decide for many
peoples; and they shall beat their swords
into plowshares, and their spears into
pruning hooks; nation shall not lift up
sword against nation, neither shall
they learn war any more." (Isaiah 2:2-4)

In Isaiah, Judaism and Christianity meet,
but diverge as well. Jews believe that
Isaiah could not have substituted his love
for Jerusalem, Zion, and his people with
an abstract love for humanity. Indeed, he is
seen as a prophet in whom both the
particular and the universal dwelled in harmony. The Messiah, whose coming at
the end of days he had prophesied, did not
signify the need to merge Jewish life
with any other church or people. On the
contrary, as a flesh-and-blood King of
Israel, the Jewish Messiah will lead his
people as the "light of the nations."

Nor will he come, Jews feel, until Israel is
restored to its place as the people of the
Messiah in the Holy Land, the Land of
Israel.

From Abraham to the Exile, in the
dreams of the Hebrew people for its restoration as a means of hastening the day of the
Messiah's coming, the land continued to
play a crucial, spiritual role. Born, cradled,
and nurtured in that land, the book
helped keep the land alive for them.

Christians look upon Isaiah as the
authentic prophetic voice that established
the divine nature of him they call
Immanuel, "God is with us" – Jesus who
was to become the Christ. In a Jerusalem valley, where the Gihon's waters
reach the so-called Garden of the
King, a mere stone's throw from the place
where Hezekiah would later fashion the
Siloam Pool, Isaiah had proclaimed to King
Ahaz the prophecy which, for Christians,
became the foundation of their faith in
Jesus as Immanuel, as the son of God who
enters history as man. And Isaiah said:
"Hear then, O house of David! . . . The
Lord himself will give you a sign. Behold, a
young woman shall conceive and bear a
son, and shall call his name Immanuel."
(Isaiah 7:13-14)

In the Christian view, the land of Israel,
with the coming of Jesus to fulfil Isaiah's
prophecies, was transformed, in the words of
Gustaf Dalman, into "the land in which
the history of Israel has achieved, in
the Person of our Lord, its aim and purpose
for humanity. Consequently, as Jesus
gathered up the significance of this land's
history into Himself, it must have been
an appropriate place for the upbringing
both of the People of God and of the
Son of Man."

28

Here, at Shechem, in the valley between Mount Gerizim and Mount Ebal, Abram came to Canaan from afar, and from the Lord, received the promise of the Land. At Shechem, the tribes of Israel were frequently reproved by their prophets.

The Roman Emperor Titus rebuilt Shechem in the year 72 of the Christian era, calling it Neapolis, or "New Town." Arabs, pronouncing "p's" as "b's," called it Nablus, the name it bears today. Nablus faces Mount Gerizim.

Samaritans, who regard Mount Gerizim as a sacred mountain, have been centred in Nablus since biblical times. Each year at Passover they ascend to the mountain's top, in ceremonial procession, to slaughter the Paschal lamb.

Samaritan Priest examining a Scroll of the Law.

Samaritan prayer service.

The Dead Sea, near whose northern end is Jericho, and at whose southern tip is Sodom, is the lowest depression on the earth's surface, its bed reaching to 792 meters below sea level. Arabs still call it "The Sea of Lot" – *Bahr Lut.*

"Lot's Wife," near the Salt Caves of Sodom. This unusual formation has been called after the poor woman who looked back, perhaps longingly, to the sinful city, "and she became a pillar of salt."

Hebron today, with its white stone houses. Dominating the town with its high, fortress-like walls is the Patriarchal sepulchre, the Cave of Machpelah, which is also sacred to Muslims as the Mosque of Abraham, the Friend – *Haram al-Khalil*.

Aerial view of the Cave of Machpelah.

At right, is Abraham's sepulchre, inside the Cave. It is richly decorated with green tapestries and embroidered with verses from the Koran and other familiar inscriptions of Muslim piety. The actual tombs of the Patriarchs and their wives are invisible. They are said to be located exactly below their respective cenotaphs, in caves that have rarely been entered since the Crusaders examined the tombs, and closed them tight.

Golden Jerusalem, majestic crown of the Holy Land, David's City, sacred to Jew, Christian and Muslim: The Jewish Temple platform atop Mount Moriah, abides in the form of the "Noble Enclosure" of the Muslims, the *Haram-es-Sharif*, with its stately Dome of the Rock, and nearby is Christianity's most sacred church, the Holy Sepulchre.

Under the Dome is the Rock on which, it is said, Abraham was to have sacrificed his son Isaac. Muslim tradition claims that Mohammed ascended to heaven from this Rock. When the Crusaders conquered Jerusalem in 1099, they transformed the mosque into a Christian shrine and called it "Templum Domini." After eighty-eight years they were banished by the Muslims.

Jacob's Well in ancient Shechem. One day Jesus stopped to rest at the foot of Mount Gerizim, in the field of Jacob. There, he asked a Samaritan woman to give him water to drink from the well. Owing to this incident, the site was made sacred by the Church, and this helped preserve Jacob's patrimony in Shechem.

Rachel's Tomb, on the road to Bethlehem. In early times, it was believed to have been shaped like a pyramid and formed of twelve stones. The Crusaders rebuilt it, erecting a square building with pointed arches over the cenotaph. Later still, in the eighteenth century, Muslims walled up the arches, thus giving the building the appearance of a typical *weli*, a tomb for a holy man, in Muslim tradition. To the west is Beit Jalla, a Christian town on the slope of a hill, where local tradition claims Mary rested on her way from Bethlehem to Ein Karem.

This site, according to tradition, is where Moses heard God speak from the Burning Bush. The Emperor Justinian built the fortress monastery now called the Monastery of St. Catherine. It was completed in 556, in the thirtieth year of his reign. Within its walls can be seen the Church of the Mother of God; Christians have always symbolically regarded Mary as the "burning bush that was not consumed."

43

Opposite page.
The rugged, almost impassable Negev mountains, through which Moses led the Israelites. They came from the wilderness of Sinai, to the wilderness of Paran, and to the wilderness of Zin, pictured here. Barren, arid, and rocky, with barely a sign of life, these are the lands which forged the national character of the Hebrews.

This page.
Site of the ancient "Walls of Jericho" where the Israelites crossed over into Canaan. Archaeological excavations here, at Tell es-Sultan, have established Jericho as the world's oldest city, dating back to at least 8000 B.C. Nearby, and seen in the background, is the Mount of Quarantine, meaning "the forty," which Jesus climbed and where he spent his forty-day fast.

Mount Tabor, one of the land's most beautiful summits, was the scene of the crucial Israelite victory over the army of Jabin, the Canaanite king, led by Sisera. Here, Deborah sang her hymn. Tabor is also believed to be the "high mountain" of the Transfiguration of Jesus.

A view of the fertile Valley of Jezreel, or the Plain of Esdraelon, from Nazareth, a city unknown in the Old Testament and first mentioned in the Gospels. The "Valley" is a great plain which lies between the hills of Nazareth to the north, Mount Tabor to the east, and the Carmel range to the south.

Tell al-Hosn, in the background, is the site of the ancient city of Beth She'an, where Philistines fastened King Saul's body to the city wall. During excavations at the Tell, archaeologists uncovered several temples. These are believed to be the "house of Ashtaroth" and the "temple of Dagon," which the Bible indicates as the place where the Philistines had put Saul's armour on public display (I Chron. 10:10). In the foreground are the excavations of a second-century Roman theatre.

Opposite page.
Mount Zion. In the foreground is the compound which includes the Christian Coenaculum, or Cenacle, and the so-called Tomb of David, erected by Muslims in the Middle Ages. The building consists of two storeys. On the lower floor is the Tomb of David; on the floor above, the "Upper Room," or the Hall of the Last Supper. This gives the name to the building, for in Latin, Coenaculum is a dining hall. The Hill of Evil Counsel can be seen in the right background.

King David's Wells, in Bethlehem. The likelihood is that these great cisterns are indeed ancient, but not from the time of David. Nevertheless, water played so vital a part in ancient times, and particularly in the military and engineering achievement of the Kings of Israel, that the popular imagination tended to link such things to them.

Opposite page left.
The "Pools of Solomon," beyond Bethlehem on the road leading to Hebron, is still another example of ancient waterworks which have been attributed to great Kings. Although Josephus says that King Solomon used to visit this place to enjoy the gardens, the hydraulic engineering involved in the construction of the Pools of Solomon is undoubtedly the product of men who lived at a period much later than the wise King.

Opposite page right.
At Megiddo, known to Christians as Armageddon – the site of the ultimate battle between the forces of good and evil – a remarkable water tunnel was built, possibly during the time of Solomon. This ingenious system insured a regular supply of fresh water for the people of Megiddo from springs outside the city walls. For a city like Megiddo, besieged so often that it became identified as a centre of warfare – thus Armageddon – such a system was particularly necessary.

The New Testament

BETHLEHEM

A mere five miles from Jerusalem, "the little town of Bethlehem" was destined to have a history and a future of its own. Although they are physically close, a range of mountains midway between the city and the town divides them. Two thousand years ago, Jerusalem was a border city of the northland, and Bethlehem the outpost of the southern region of Judah, the most northern site of David's tribeland. Bethlehem, birthplace of this great King, was a place of herds, but it also deserved its name, "The House of Bread," for on the plain below its mountain range, there stretched forth deep-earthed arable lands, most unusual for this rocky region.

The story of Ruth and Boaz, as detailed in the Old Testament, is set in Bethlehem, and it is morally fitting that Ruth, who descended from one of Israel's mortal enemies, the fierce Moabites, should have become, through her marriage to Boaz, the great grandmother of King David, defender of his people, yet founder of the Messianic House of David. In and near Bethlehem, David triumphed over the Philistines, arch-enemies of Israel and Judah. In the spiritual history of Christianity, Bethlehem is the place of the Nativity because it was the first City of David.

"And in that region there were shepherds out in the field, keeping watch over their flock by night." (Luke 2:8) Christian tradition has linked "Shepherds' Field" with the Fields of Ruth and Boaz, as described in the Old Testament Book of Ruth. In these fields, according to tradition, "An angel of the Lord appeared to them . . . and suddenly there was with the angel a multitude of the heavenly host praising God and saying 'Glory to God in the highest, and on earth peace among men with whom he is pleased!' " (Luke 2:9; 14)

It was a decree of Caesar Augustus, commanding a census of all the provinces under the sway of the Romans, that brought Mary and Joseph to their native town. The birth of the Christian saviour in Bethlehem was to give the town an eternal appeal in the lives of men and in the histories of nations. Luke records the events:

"In those days a decree went out from Caesar Augustus that all the world should be enrolled. This was the first enrollment . . . and all went to be enrolled, each to his own city. And Joseph also went up from Galilee, from the city of Nazareth, to Judea, to the city of David, which is called Bethlehem, because he was of the house and lineage of David, to be enrolled with Mary, his betrothed, who was with child. And while they were there, the time came for her to be delivered. And she gave birth to her first-born son and wrapped him in swaddling clothes, and laid him in a manger, because there was no place for them in the inn. And in that region there were shepherds out in the field, keeping watch over their flock by night. And an angel of the Lord appeared to them, and the glory of the Lord shone around them, and they were filled with fear. And the angel said to them, 'Be not afraid; for behold, I bring you good news of a great joy which will come to all the people; for to you is born this day in the city of David a Savior, who is Christ the Lord.' " (Luke 2:1-13)

Opposite page.
The "Pillars of Solomon," deep in the southern Negev Desert, stand guard over the King's copper mines at Timna. From the nearby port of Elath, copper ingots were shipped eastward, and in return, goods of value and beauty came to the land.

After the unsuccessful Jewish war with the Romans, not only did Jerusalem come under the dominion of the expanding pagan Empire, but Bethlehem fell too, and Jews were excluded from both places. The Roman cult was undoubtedly carried on in Bethlehem as it was in Aeolia Capitolina, which is what the Roman emperors called the old Jewish capital of Jerusalem.

Then, in the year 325, a Council of the Church met in Asia Minor, in the city of Nicea. At the so-called Nicean Council, the Bishop of Jerusalem, Bishop Macarius, took advantage of the opportunity to confide to the Emperor Constantine, who was a new convert to Christianity, concerning the neglected and forsaken condition of the various holy places in his diocese. It was not long thereafter that the Emperor himself undertook to erect three monumental churches commemorating the principal events of the life of Jesus: his birth, his death, and his ascension. Thus there rose important basilicas in Bethlehem, commemorating the Nativity; in Jerusalem, at the Holy Sepulchre near Calvary; and the Ascension, on the Mount of Olives.

Over the centuries, more and more Christians began to make pilgrimages to Bethlehem. As interest developed, local inhabitants satisfied the pious longings and curiosities of those who had come from so far afield to venerate the town. Additional "sacred" sites were added: the place where the Magi dismounted was located, the well in which their star had fallen was pointed out, and other such "popular beliefs" were encouraged. In spite of the overgrowth of such "sites," Bethlehem's spiritual greatness was still centred principally in the Nativity, and in the old and venerated Grotto where the Christian saviour came into history and the world.

NAZARETH

Nazareth's holiest place is the Annunciation, the site of the Angel Gabriel's announcement to Mary, as recorded in the first chapter of Luke, that she would give birth to Jesus:

"In the sixth month the angel Gabriel was sent from God to the city of Galilee named Nazareth, to a virgin betrothed to a man whose name was Joseph, of the house of David; and the virgin's name was Mary. And he came to her and said, 'Hail, O favored one, the Lord is with you! . . . And behold, you will conceive in your womb and bear a son, and you shall call his name Jesus. He will be great, and will be called the Son of the Most High; and the Lord will give to him the throne of his father David. . . .' " (Luke 1:26-32)

Although such sites as that of the Annunciation are venerated by tradition and are significant in the history of Nazareth, the city will always be known as the boyhood home of Jesus. Nazareth tells us much about the way Jesus came to think and to preach.

Here biblical history unfolds before one's very eyes. Here Jesus grew into manhood, and here his eyes were opened up to his people's past. He liked to retire to the mountains for prayer. The Mount of Olives in Jerusalem was, for him, as fitting a place for meditation as the Temple itself. On lonely heights in Nazareth, he meditated. As he cast his eyes in all directions, he could not help but respond to a landscape fraught with historical memories.

To the east, in the forest areas – important for the carpenter of Nazareth – was the round and majestic height of Tabor, where Barak had rushed down to the plain (Judges 4:6-12). To the southeast, hidden by some small peaks, he could see the battlefield of Gideon and recall his victories (Judges 7:1). In the further distance could be seen the mountains of Gilboa, where Saul, Israel's first King, had met his tragic death (I Samuel 31:4). And he could recall to mind the memory of Josiah, the last of the God-reverencing Kings of Judah, whose death he could picture at Megiddo (II Kings 23:29). Looking westward, he could see the Carmel mountain range. No viewer of these heights could look upon them without remembering Elijah the Prophet, who had carried out his battles there, against the false prophets of Baal (I Kings 18:21).

In 1880, the well-known historical geographer George Adam Smith, climbed the 1,500 meters of Nazareth's hill and wrote: "Esdraelon lies before you . . . to the east, the Valley of the Jordan with the long range of Gilead; to the west, the radiance of the Great Sea, with the ships of Tarshish and the promise of the Isles. You see thirty miles in three directions. It is a map of Old Testament history."

Nazareth, thus, is a place that touches upon the history of the Jews for "history is seen" from its heights. It is not an out-of-the-way tiny town, tucked away and hidden in Galilee. Its openness to the wide horizons surrounding it, to the valleys below, the lands around, and the seas beyond – these surely must have contributed to Jesus' universal views, and to his interest in the affairs and destiny of other nations, in addition to those of his own people.

Indeed, not always did his views coincide with those of his fellow Jews. From time to time, he would stand up amongst them, in the synagogues of Galilee, where he joined them for regular Sabbath worship, and his discourse on interpretations of older traditions would not always please his listeners. But this, indeed, was the fate of all the bold among the ancient Jewish teachers and prophets. Often their courageous reinterpretations of earlier views did not meet with easy public reception, and they, like Jesus in the Nazareth synagogue, must also have had occasion to exclaim: "Truly, I say to you, no prophet is acceptable in his own country." (Luke 4:24)

CANA OF GALILEE

Jesus' miracle-working proved to be a double-edged sword. Among the general populace these seemingly divine attributes and talents brought him favour and fame, but the established religious leadership tended to regard them as the working of magic. "Can anything good come out of Nazareth?" (John 1:46) Thus asks Nathanael, an Israelite, reflecting the mood of many of his people. Nathanael, whose home was in the fortified town of Cana in Galilee, not only looked with disdain upon Nazareth itself but also upon those who came from there. That is what made the miracle Jesus performed at Cana so very significant, for "This, the first of his signs, Jesus did in Cana in Galilee, and manifested his glory; and his disciples believed in him." (John 2:11)

Kfar Kana lies four miles northeast of Nazareth on the road to Tiberias, the Cana of Galilee of the New Testament story. There took place in Cana a miracle: water made into wine.

"On the third day there was a marriage at Cana in Galilee, and the mother of Jesus was there; Jesus also was invited to the marriage, with his disciples. When the wine failed, the mother of Jesus said to him, 'They have no wine. . . .' His mother said to the servants, 'Do whatever he tells you.' Now six stone jars were standing there, for the Jewish rites of purification, each holding two or three measures. Jesus said to them, 'Fill the jars with water.' And they filled them up to the brim. He said to them, 'Now draw some out and take it to the steward for the feast.' So they took it. When the steward of the feast tasted the water now become wine . . . [he] did not know where it came from. . . ." (John 2:1-10)

AT THE JORDAN

The Jordan river is a small stream with a long and unending history. For Christians, it is a sacred river because in its waters Jesus was baptized by John the Baptist.

"In those days came John the Baptist, preaching in the wilderness of Judea, 'Repent, for the kingdom of heaven is at hand.' For this is he who was spoken of by the prophet Isaiah when he said, 'The voice of one crying in the wilderness: Prepare the way of the Lord, make his paths straight.' . . . Then Jesus came from Galilee to the Jordan to John, to be baptized by him." (Matthew 3:1-13)

The Jordan starts with four streams at the foot of Mount Hermon – the Banias, the Dan, the Baraghit, and the Hasbani. At its sources it begins at a height of about 2,800 feet, and then, in the course of its flow some eight miles southward to Lake Huleh, it falls to 2,500 feet. It then cascades through a basalt gorge, and in the eleven miles of its flow farther south to the Sea of Galilee, it continues to fall another thousand feet.

The Jordan is a swift and fierce stream at places, a quiet almost apathetic river else-where. Indeed, it deserves its name *Yarden*, the "Descender," or "the river that goes down." It flows for 233 miles, leaving behind the perpetual snows of Mt. Hermon at altitudes of almost nine thousand feet, and then twisting its way down to the depths of the Dead Sea, to the earth's lowest surface.

As the Jordan descends it becomes more and more saline, and its evaporation leads to extensive mineral deposits. It is not always the most inviting of waterways. Indeed, unlike most of the world's rivers, it has never served as a link but only as a barrier, for it has remained unnavigable. Nevertheless, the river has been hospitable to man. In the Jordan Valley, just south of the Sea of Galilee, at Ubeidye, a prehistorical skull, believed to be about a half-million years old, was discovered in 1959. For all its strangeness as a river, it is entirely likely that man's oldest sedentary inhabitations began on or near the banks of the Jordan.

SEA OF GALILEE

The Sea of Galilee, with fertile plateaus on its east and west shores, is nevertheless encased by slopes beyond that stand around the lake like high and mighty walls. Its blue surface is thus set within a green frame. Fed partly by natural springs, it is mostly endowed by the Jordan's flow, streaming down to it from the north.

The Sea of Galilee is sometimes called "the Lake of Jesus" since he performed so many miracles within its immediate environment. From Nazareth, Jesus transferred his dwelling-place to the vicinity of Capernaum, at the side of the sea, where he hoped to find a more receptive group for his teachings. He was not disappointed. Several natives of this district attached themselves to him: Simon (Peter) and Andrew, James and John.

"As he walked by the Sea of Galilee, he saw two brothers, Simon who is called Peter and Andrew his brother, casting a net into the sea; for they were fishermen. And he said to them, 'Follow me, and I will make you fishers of men.' . . . And going on from there he saw two other brothers, James the son of Zebedee and John his brother, in the boat with Zebedee their father, mending nets, and he called them. Immediately they left the boat and their father, and followed him." (Matthew 4:18-22)

Thus, at the Sea of Galilee, his first permanent disciples joined him.

Before long, there were Twelve Disciples – symbolically, one from each of the twelve tribes of Israel – to represent the inclusion of the whole of his people as part of his new community. He gave them "power and authority over all demons, and to cure diseases, and he sent them out to preach the kingdom of God and to heal." (Luke 9:1-2)

One day, upon their return from their missionary journeys among the people, a miracle took place, not very far from Capernaum, on the north shore of the Sea of Galilee. Tabgha is the traditional site of the story of the loaves and the fishes. At this place, tradition has it, the disciples met with Jesus to give him reports of their travels and achievements, at what was clearly to have been an intimate private discussion between master and disciples.

But the local inhabitants pressed in on Jesus and he received them "and cured those who had need of healing." The disciples, as the day began to wear on, urged that the multitudes be sent away "to go into the villages and country round about, to lodge and get provisions" for they had no food to eat in that "lonely place." Yet Jesus refused. "You give them something to eat," he said.

"They said, 'We have no more than five loaves and two fish – unless we are to go to and buy food for all these people.' For there were about five thousand men. And he said to his disciples, 'Make them sit down in companies, about fifty each.' And they did so, and made them all sit down. And taking the five loaves and the two fish he looked up to heaven, and blessed and broke them, and gave them to the disciples to set before the crowd. And all ate and were satisfied. And they took up what was left over, twelve baskets of broken pieces." (Luke 9:13-17)

MOUNT OF BEATITUDES

Christianity, to be sure, is the faith of those who believe in Jesus as Messiah. To Christians, Jesus is not only a Saviour but also a Teacher. Jesus was raised in the midst of his people, and the very cast of his language as well as the shape of his thoughts witness his Jewish life, learning, and religious tradition. Therefore, his words to the multitudes of his people, as he "went up into a mountain" near Capernaum, close by Tabgha, and within clear view of the Sea of Galilee, must always be remembered and carefully placed within the proper context: "Think not," he said, "that I have come to abolish the law and the prophets; I have come not to abolish them but to fulfil them. For truly, I say to you, till heaven and earth pass away, not one iota, not a dot, will pass from the law until all is accomplished." (Matthew 5:17-18).

These words rang down from the mountain, the place that has since come to be called the Mount of Beatitudes. Looking over the lake's waters, he spoke forth words and thoughts taken straight out of his Old Testament background – words that could surely be heard distinctly below, at the foot of the mountain. The words of the Sermon on the Mount live forever.

"Seeing the crowds, he went up on the mountain, and when he sat down his disciples came to him. And he opened his mouth and taught them, saying:
Blessed are the poor in spirit, for theirs is the kingdom of heaven.
Blessed are those who mourn, for they shall be comforted.
Blessed are the meek, for they shall inherit the earth.
Blessed are those who hunger and thirst for righteousness, for they shall be satisfied.
Blessed are the merciful, for they shall obtain mercy.

Blessed are the pure in heart, for they shall
see God.
Blessed are the peacemakers, for they shall
be called sons of God.
Blessed are those who are persecuted for
righteousness' sake; for theirs is the
kingdom of heaven.
Blessed are you when men revile you and
persecute you and utter all kinds of evil
against you falsely on my account.
Rejoice and be glad, for your reward is
great in heaven, for so men persecuted
the prophets who were before you."

(Matthew 5: 1-12)

Little wonder that the Sea of Galilee,
which Jesus faced on the mountain as he
spoke forth these immemorial words,
remains sacred to Christians. Little wonder,
too, that Jews who listen to these New
Testament words can hear their familiar
Old Testament accents and the resound-
ing echoes of older prophets.

ENTRY INTO JERUSALEM

Like every other member of the Jewish
community, Jesus loved Jerusalem. It was
the capital of his nation – the City of
David. It was the seat of the Temple on
Mount Moriah. True, Jesus despised
the evil-doing of some priests in their
Temple dealings. The emphasis of his
teachings was on the ethical act, the pious
deed, and not the empty rote ritual
alone. In these views, he was not at odds
with most of his teachers, the Rabbinical
Pharisees, who similarly taught that a man's
faith can be tested principally by the way in
which he relates to his fellow man. "Thou
shalt love the Lord thy God," they taught;
and, like Jesus, they too emphasized the
need man has to "love thy neighbor as
thyself."

In the words of the Gospel, one "goes
up" to Jerusalem. This was the way
Jews thought of their capital city. "Going
up to Jerusalem" in the Old Testament
was not merely a description of a physical
ascent, but also of a spiritual arrival.
Jesus' parents went up to Jerusalem "every
year at the feast of the Passover. And
when he was twelve years old, they went
up according to custom . . . the boy
Jesus stayed behind in Jerusalem . . .
after three days they found him in the
temple, sitting among the teachers,
listening to them and asking them ques-
tions; and all who heard him were
amazed at his understanding and his
answers." (Luke 2:41-47).

Indeed, years later, when he was grown
into manhood, his last week on earth
was spent in the area of Jerusalem, for it
was the eve of Passover, and he "went
up" to the Temple.

THE MOUNT OF OLIVES

To celebrate the Passover in the capital city
of Jerusalem, in the Temple precincts,
Jesus travelled southward to Jericho,
thence across the dry stretches of the
wilderness up to Jerusalem. From the low-
lying distance, as one climbs upward to
Jerusalem, the Mount of Olives is clearly
seen. He arrived at Bethany, close by the
Mount of Olives.

"And when they drew near to Jerusalem and came to Bethphage, to the Mount of Olives, then Jesus sent two disciples, saying to them, 'Go into the village opposite you, and immediately you will find an ass tied, and a colt with her; untie them and bring them to me . . .' This took place to fulfil what was spoken by the prophet, saying, 'Tell the daughter of Zion, Behold, your king is coming to you, humble, and mounted on an ass, and on a colt, the foal of an ass. . . .' Most of the crowd spread their clothes on the road, and others cut branches from the trees and spread them on the road. And the crowds that went before him and that followed him shouted, 'Hosanna to the Son of David! Blessed be he who comes in the name of the Lord! Hosanna in the highest!' And when he entered Jerusalem, all the city was stirred, saying, 'Who is this?' And the crowds said, 'This is the prophet Jesus from Nazareth of Galilee.' " (Matthew 21:1-11)

To Jews, the Mount of Olives is a sacred place. From very early days in the popular mind it has played an important role in the coming of the Messiah. An old mystical commentary contains these words: "The Messiah, the son of David, and Elijah and Zerubbabel, peace be unto them, ascend to the summit of the Mount of Olives. And the Messiah will command Elijah to blow the ram's horn. At the fourth blast, the mountains will turn into plains and the entire surface of the earth will become level."

Thus not for naught did Jews from very early times select the Mount of Olives as a burial place. When the Messiah's horn blew, the dead would arise, so the legend taught, and go to Mount Moriah, to the Temple Mount, where the Presence of God would receive them. To be buried within the walls was forbidden; thus to face the city walls from the Mount of Olives was to be as close as possible.

To Christians, the Mount of Olives is the most holy of all places in the land. Here Jesus taught his disciples how to pray; here he looked out upon the city and sorrowfully wept over what he saw on the horizon, the future destruction of his beloved Jerusalem at the hands of the Romans. And, most important of all, from here, at the summit, he ascended to heaven.

LAST DAYS

"For the Almighty did not redeem our ancestors alone, but us, as well," so prayed the Jews of Jesus' day at Passover time. The Feast of Unleavened Bread left its imprint on every facet of Jewish religious life. Every Sabbath, the Exodus from Egypt is recalled. And on every major festival of the year there is a remembrance of the wonderful deliverance which God wrought for the Israelites when he redeemed them from Egypt.

Christianity may be said to have its roots in the Jewish Passover too, but it has become something quite different. Many scholars believe that the Last Supper held in the Upper Room was, in fact, a Passover ritual meal, and that the "bread of affliction" – the unleavened bread, or *matzot*, which Jews eat and ritually remember on that occasion – was to be transformed by Jesus into something altogether new for those who followed him.

"And when he had given thanks, he broke it, and said, 'This is my body which is broken for you. Do this in remembrance of me.' " (I Corinthians 11:24) Thus the Last Supper marks a new beginning. The cup which all disciples of Jesus ever since bless, and the bread which they break – in remembrance of the words he spoke to all who would follow him – abide forever. In a time of trouble and subjection, the recall of the first redemption on the Passover, awakened the thought of a new redemption through a new testament which the God of Israel might yet perform.

Essentially, it was from the yoke of Rome, her emperors and procurators, that Jesus sought redemption. When he wept, on the Mount of Olives, it was because he foresaw the destruction Rome was yet to bring against his beloved people and city. Now, by the mystery of language and faith at the Last Supper, he foresaw the redemption that was yet to come through the Father, the Lord God of Israel. As Isaac was to be sacrificed, so now was he. "This is my body," "this is my blood," he said, pointing to the bread and the wine at the Passover meal.

GARDEN OF GETHSEMANE

From the Upper Room where he celebrated the Last Supper, in mystical and ceremonial fashion, Jesus went to the Garden of Gethsemane on the Mount of Olives. He came down with his disciples into the Kidron Valley, the very same way David, centuries earlier, had traversed when he had fled from Absalom.

Gethsemane, the place to which Jesus had repaired to spend his last night, is known in Hebrew as *Gat Shemanim,* the place of the "oil-press." The Garden of Gethsemane has been designated as the place where Jesus prayed before the passion. Here, to this day, several very ancient olive trees may still be found. Some botanists have claimed that their age may, indeed, be over three thousand years old.

Upon the very site, which tradition maintains that Jesus made sacred by his prayer and agony on the evening preceding his passion and death, a church was built in the time of Theodosius, toward the end of the fourth century. Today a modern church, the Basilica of the Agony, is to be found there. Since so many nations around the world helped to build this new Basilica, it has also acquired the name of the Church of All Nations.

VIA DOLOROSA

During the period of the First Temple, in the days of Solomon, the city gate of Jerusalem, from the eastern side, was known as the Sheep Gate. Jesus entered the city from the Garden of Gethsemane via these gates. Today they are called either Lions' Gate or St. Stephen's Gate. The road he trod from the Pretorium, where he received his sentence, to Calvary is called the Way of Sorrows, the Via Dolorosa. Along this sorrowful way, fourteen stations have been prescribed, based on the Gospel narrative as well as on centuries-old traditions. At each of these stations from the Pretorium to Calvary, a number or an inscription recalls a poignant moment in his last tragic hour, as Jesus walked toward the bare and rocky summit. Known from the Latin word for "bald" as *Calvary*, or as *Golgotha*, from the Hebrew and Aramaic word for "skull," such bare rock formations, many of which may still be found in the environs of Jerusalem, had undoubtedly suggested a bald, skull-like image.

The fourteen Stations of the Cross are:
1. Jesus is condemned to death.
2. Jesus receives the Cross.
3. Jesus falls the first time.
4. Jesus meets his afflicted mother.
5. Simon of Cyrene helps Jesus carry his Cross.
6. Veronica wipes the face of Jesus.
7. Jesus falls the second time.
8. Jesus speaks to the daughters of Jerusalem.
9. Jesus falls the third time.
10. Jesus is stripped of his garments.
11. Jesus is nailed to the Cross.
12. Jesus dies on the Cross.
13. Jesus is taken down from the Cross.
14. Jesus is laid in the Sepulchre.

THE HOLY SEPULCHRE

Joseph of Arimathaea owned a family sepulchre, in a garden close by the Hill of Calvary. It was not permitted, according to Jewish religious custom, to bury the dead within the city, but only outside the city's walls. Indeed, even today, a visitor to Jerusalem will note that a number of cemeteries and mausoleums, principally Jewish and Muslim, ring the outer rim of the city's walls, virtually surrounding the old city.

"Now there was a man named Joseph from the Jewish town of Arimathaea . . . this man went to Pilate and asked for the body of Jesus. Then he took it down and wrapped it in a linen shroud, and laid him in a rock-hewn tomb, where no one had ever yet been laid." (Luke 23:50-53)

The Tomb in which Jesus was laid was typical of Jewish graves of the time. It was composed, in effect, of two rooms, one leading to the other by means of a door that opened between. The first room served as an antechamber. There the family would gather to mourn their dead. The second was the actual sepulchre, a couch cut into the rock into which the body was laid.

Then, after the interment in the rock, the entrance to the burial rooms was closed by means of a large millstone, which was made to fit over the opening.

The narrative in the Gospels surely accords with these Jewish burial customs and styles. According to the Gospel account it was possible to enter the sepulchre and yet be in front of the entrance to the tomb. Indeed, it is most striking that, in the very spot where it was believed that the tomb of Jesus should be sought, a tomb corresponding in every detail with the description given in the Gospels was actually found. Indeed, it is near the family sepulchre believed to have belonged to Joseph of Arimathaea, yet by its very isolation from these other graves it seems to point to its own uniqueness as a special grave used only by Jesus and no other.

Emperor Hadrian, the powerful pagan Roman king who wished to curtail both Judaism and Christianity, forbade the Jews the teaching of the Torah (the Pentateuch and the Prophets) and also prevented them from engaging in certain religious practices like the rite of circumcision. He was equally harsh on Christians. Indeed, as both a symbol of his contempt for their religion and a sign of his practical desire to wipe out their historic atttachments to the Holy Land, he constructed a pagan temple to Venus on the very site of Calvary. A Roman forum was erected nearby. Even the name of Jerusalem was changed by Hadrian to Aeolia Capitolina. Jews and Christians of Jewish origin were forbidden access to Aeolia.

Two centuries had to elapse before a new and revolutionary development would occur, bringing to Jerusalem something of its older glory and centrality. When Constantine, the first Christian Emperor of Rome, met Bishop Macarius of Jerusalem, the latter was given imperial permission to carry out excavations beneath the Forum of Aeolia and the Temple of Venus. Eusebius, a native of Palestine and a recognized historian, has described what happened:

"The Emperor ordered that this place should be cleansed . . . immediately the order was received, these edifices which had been erected by fraud were thrown to the ground from their full height and the seats of false gods were deprived and purged of their statues . . . the basic soil was uncovered at last and, in the bowels of the earth, the venerable and truly holy witness to the resurrection of the Saviour was revealed against all hope, and the discovery of the cavern, the new Holy of Holies, was a striking confirmation of the saviour's return to life."

Immediately Constantine made available the funds necessary for the construction of a basilica: "It is your task," he told Macarius, "to ensure that everything is done in order that this edifice shall be not only the most beautiful in the world but that all the details of its decoration will outdo in magnificence the splendors of the greatest cities."

Indeed, the Emperor's mother, Queen Helena, whom some have half-seriously called the world's first archaeologist, came to Jerusalem in person – the first time a high Roman official baptized into the Christian faith had shown such great concern in the life and work of the Church.

Her arrival in Jerusalem at an advanced age stirred the interest and the enthusiasm of the local population; indeed, Bishop Macarius went to receive her at the head of a stately procession. The Church of the Holy Sepulchre had been planned before her trip to the Holy Land, but two other basilicas – the one atop the Mount of Olives, which she knew as the Mount of Ascension, and the other at the site of the Nativity, in Bethlehem – were built and planned by her. She did not long survive her triumphal sojourn in the Holy Land, for shortly after her return to Constantinople, in 327 or 328, she died.

Bishop Macarius presided at the inauguration ceremonies held at the completion of the Church of the Holy Sepulchre, in 335. This great building was destroyed in 614, then rebuilt. Again, in 1010, it was destroyed by the Caliph Hakim and rebuilt thereafter.

The edifice Constantine had built was more than a church for it consisted of a whole group of buildings. The Crusaders conceived the idea of taking all the buildings, uniting them into one, and making a new monumental basilica in the form of a cross. For several centuries thereafter, as a result of the care and concern of the Franciscans, who took over the Holy Places on behalf of the Roman Catholic Church after the Crusaders left, the Holy Sepulchre was restored and preserved. In 1808, a disastrous fire virtually destroyed the rotunda of the church,

and the Greek Orthodox Church then undertook to make the necessary repairs.

What has been called the "Status Quo" of the holy places, and particularly the rights of the various Christian communities in the Holy Sepulchre, goes back to the year 1757. The Sultan of Turkey issued an edict, subsequently reaffirmed in 1852, defining the holy places of the Christians, and the rights of each Christian denomination in them, as well as the principal shrines of the Muslims and the Jews. The Holy Sepulchre thus has been principally the joint property of three denominations – the Greek Orthodox, the Latin (Roman Catholic), and the Armenian. Additionally, the Copts, Syrians, and Abyssinians have certain limited rights and property within the Church. Peace, unfortunately, has not always reigned within the Holy Sepulchre, as a result of so many "landlords" sharing the same area, often at the very same time.

Since the year 1246, complicated rules have governed the opening and closing of the doors of the Church of the Holy Sepulchre. The façade still preserves the Crusader architecture with its twin doors. One door has been closed since the time of Saladin, while the other has been placed in the custody of two Muslim families. One of these families is the "keeper of the key" to the door; the other family has the privilege and responsibility of opening the door. The lock to the door is placed so high up it can be reached only with the aid of a ladder. Bells hung behind the door announce the opening of the door and peal out the arrival of the processions and solemn entrances of the various Christian communities who have rights within.

The Nave of the Basilica of the Nativity. To commemorate the place of Jesus' birth, the Roman Emperor Constantine, a pagan convert to Christianity, undertook to erect the Basilica of the Nativity. The builders were guided by local residents, who kept sacred the cave in which Jesus was born.

In 527, Justinian became emperor of the Byzantine Empire, and among his great expansive acts on behalf of the churches throughout the Empire was his complete rebuilding of Constantine's Basilica at Bethlehem. Since that time the essential form of the Church has not been altered. Of the mosaics which decorated the Basilica in the twelfth century, only a few fragments remain on the north and south walls.

Opposite page.
Directly below the Basilica's high altar is the Grotto of the Nativity, with its altar located on the exact site of the birth. "Here was born Jesus Christ of the Virgin Mary" – *Hic de Virgine Maria Jesus Christus Natus Est.* This inscription is fitted into the floor of the altar and surrounded by a vermillion star, seen on the left. It is in the hands of the Greek Orthodox Church. To the right, on the grotto's north side, is the Chapel of the Manger of the Roman Catholics, commemorating the Scriptural description of Mary, who "wrapped him up in swaddling clothes and laid him in a manger."

"And behold, you will conceive in your womb and bear a son, and you shall call his name Jesus. . . ." Thus spoke the Angel Gabriel to Mary in Nazareth, announcing the forthcoming birth. We see here the recently built Church of the Annunciation, erected above the grotto where Gabriel appeared before Mary. In Galilean Nazareth, Jesus grew to manhood, and from the heights of Nazareth the Jewish history he knew and experienced unfolded before his eyes: the Valley of Esdraelon below, the Jordan Valley to the east, and the Great Sea, with its ships to Tarshish, to the west.

Mary's Well, not far from the site of the Annunciation, is traditionally regarded as the place where Mary herself came regularly for water when she lived in Narazeth. Modernization has come to Nazareth and plumbing has brought taps and faucets to many families; still, some women and children continue the custom of centuries, and draw water here for their families.

The Chapel of the Greek Orthodox Church built at the site of Mary's Well at Nazareth.

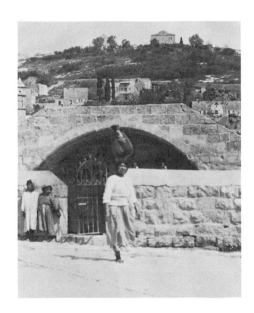

In Nazareth and in other places in the Galilean north, Jesus prayed in the synagogues of his day. Indeed, he preached there as well. Here, on the site of one such synagogue in Nazareth, is a Melkite Church, a congregation of Greek-Catholic Christian Arabs who today number about 25,000 and constitute one of the larger Christian denominations in the Holy Land. This church is known as the "Synagogue-Church," for it is believed to be the actual site where Jesus preached as described in the fourth chapter of Luke: "And he said to them, 'Doubtless you will quote to me this proverb, "Physician, heal yourself . . ."' And he said, 'Truly, I say to you, no prophet is acceptable in his own country. . . .' When they heard this, all in the synagogue were filled with wrath. And they rose up and put him out of the city, and led him to the brow of the hill on which their city was built, that they might throw him down headlong." (Luke 4:23 ff.)

"The Mount of the Leap of the Lord," shown this page, is the traditional site of the "brow of the hill." But Jesus passed through, and went on his way, unharmed, to teach in the synagogue of Capernaum.

The synagogue at Capernaum, on the northern edge of the Sea of Galilee. Here, "on the sabbath he entered the synagogue and taught." (Mark 1:21) Capernaum is the Greek spelling of the Hebrew name, Kfar Nahum – the Village of Nahum. The ruins of the second- or third-century synagogue are believed to be very close to the Jewish house of prayer which existed in the days of Jesus, and where he preached and taught.

Still in a relatively good state of preservation at the site are decorated arches, sculptured capitals, carved lintels and stone benches for worshippers. The Ark, which contained the sacred Scrolls of the Law – from which Jesus must have read, and upon whose teachings he based his homilies – was oriented in the direction of Jerusalem, and thus stood on the south wall of the nave.

Here, in a tiny hamlet, Ein Karem, the "spring of the vineyard," four miles west of Jerusalem, John the Baptist was born. In these Judaean hillsides, John spent his early years before he "went into all the region about the Jordan, preaching a baptism of repentance for the forgiveness of sins." (Luke 3:3) The name Ein Karem is not mentioned in the Gospel, but Christian tradition, supported by archaeological findings and literary documents, makes it clear that it is, indeed, the place of John's birth. In the Middle Ages, in fact, Ein Karem's name was changed by the Crusaders to "St. John in the Mountains."

The Jordan River: a small stream with an unending history. It is sacred to Christians because in its waters Jesus was baptized by John the Baptist. It flows for 233 miles, from its source in the north fed by Mount Hermon's perpetual snows, twisting and turning its way down to the depths of the Dead Sea, the earth's lowest surface.

The Sea of Galilee has many names. In the Old Testament books of Numbers and Deuteronomy, it is called Kinneret, which in Hebrew means harp. Some believe this name was given because the sea is shaped like the harp; others because of a legend which describes its gentle waters lapping against the shores "as sweet as the voice of the harp." In the New Testament, it is called the Sea of Galilee, the Sea of Tiberias or Lake of Tiberias, and the Lake or the Sea of Gennesaret. It is often regarded by Christians as the "Lake of Jesus," since he performed so many miracles in its vicinity. This page we see the city of Tiberias, with the Tomb of Rabbi Meir the Miracle-Worker near the shore.

Opposite page.
The "first of his signs, Jesus did at Cana in Galilee, and manifested his glory; and his disciples believed in him." (John 2:11) Attending a marriage feast in Cana, and seeing that there was no wine, Jesus made the water into wine. Cana has since been identified not only as the place where Jesus publicly performed a miracle but also as the place where, by his presence, he raised marriage to the dignity of a sacrament. In 1879, the Franciscans built the Parish Church of Cana, on the remains of a sixth-century sanctuary.

Facing the Sea of Galilee is
the Mount of Beatitudes,
atop which Jesus spoke these
well-known and immortal
words, words steeped in his
own Hebraic tradition:
"Blessed are the poor in
spirit . . . Blessed are those
who mourn . . . Blessed are
the meek . . . Blessed are
the peacemakers . . ." In
1937, the Franciscans built
the Church of the Beatitudes
atop the Mount to mark the
site.

Jesus wept over Jerusalem as he viewed it from the Mount of Olives. He foresaw the destruction of the city he loved. "And he was now drawing near, at the descent of the Mount of Olives . . . And when he . . . saw the city he wept over it, saying, '. . . For the days shall come upon you, when your enemies will cast up a bank about you, and surround you, and hem you in on every side . . .'" (Luke 19:37 ff.)

The site of his weeping over Jerusalem remained unmarked until the time of the Crusaders who built a church there, which later fell into ruins. Today, a modern church stands on this site. It was designed by Antonio Barluzzi, whose devotion to the restoration and rebuilding of Christian shrines throughout the Holy Land was matched only by his artistic genius. It is known as "Dominus Flevit" – The Lord Wept.

Opposite page.
The procession re-enacting Jesus' arrival in Jerusalem moves from Bethphage, on the eastern slope of the Mount of Olives, crosses the crest of the hill, then passes through Gethsemane, into the walled city, through its eastern gate. The faithful chant as they march, bearing palm and olive branches in their hands.

This page.
The Mount of Olives is perhaps most important to Christians as the site from where Jesus ascended to heaven. To mark the spot, a church was erected there in 387 by a pious Roman lady. A few foundations of the outer wall still exist from this building. In 1187, the Church of the Ascension was made into a mosque. The cupola and arcades built by the Muslims still remain. The Church of the Ascension is one of the seven official Christian holy places in the Holy Land which are recognized in international law.

To the right is the Tower of the Russian Compound, its 214 steps and six storeys visible for many miles to the east and the south. This church stands on the foundations of one built in the fourth century. The head of John the Baptist was supposedly found there at the time of Constantine.

Excavations have unearthed a street with steps which led down from the Upper Chamber, the Cenacle, to the Pool of Siloam. These are probably the very steps which Jesus traversed on Holy Thursday night, when he repaired to the Garden of Gethsemane, after his Last Supper with his disciples.

"The Upper Room" in Jerusalem, where Jesus celebrated the Last Supper. Known as the Coenacle – dining hall in Latin – it is located in the same building as a Muslim mosque and cenotaph that Muslims had erected to the memory of King David, and which has been popularly regarded, ever since, as "David's Tomb."

The Garden of Gethsemane, profuse with its olive trees, is situated at the foot of the Mount of Olives. "And they went to a place called Gethsemane; and he said to his disciples, 'Sit here, while I pray.'" (Mark 14:32)

In this lovely garden, with its garlands and flowers, Jesus was betrayed. Ironically, it was in Gethsemane, where he had spent good days before, that the ordeal of his last twenty-four hours on earth commenced.

The Rock of Agony – the place made sacred by the prayer and agony of Jesus on Thursday evening, preceding his Passion and Death. "And he took with him Peter and James and John, and began to be greatly distressed and troubled. And he said to them, 'My soul is very sorrowful, even to death; remain here, and watch.' And going a little farther, he fell on the ground and prayed that, if it were possible, the hour might pass from him." (Mark 14:33-35) Overlooking the Valley of Kidron, the Rock of Agony is enclosed today in a beautiful modern church known as the Church of all Nations.

A unique landmark overlooking the Kidron Valley, on the slopes of the Mount of Olives, is the Russian Church of St. Mary Magdalene, consecrated in 1888. It has seven golden onion-shaped cupolas. Below the church in the garden are parts of the ancient stairs of the way from the city of Jerusalem to the top of the Mount of Olives. Many old Jewish tombs may also be found on the grounds.

The Church of the Assumption, at the foot of the Mount of Olives, stands on the site of the "Tomb of Virgin Mary." From this tomb, some Christians have believed, Mary was taken into heaven; she was not subject to the yoke of sin and so bore none of its consequences. In the background is Mount Scopus. Old olive trees, similar to those in the nearby Garden of Gethsemane, are visible in the foreground.

On Good Friday each year, the Via Dolorosa is crowded with worshippers who piously bear the Cross as Jesus did, moving from the first to the very last station, which is within the Sepulchre itself.

In the time of Constantine, when the Church of the Holy Sepulchre was built, Calvary stood outside the Church, set apart within a separate courtyard. The Crusaders expanded the Church itself, and included the four last stations – all the sacred rites and monuments of Calvary itself – within the Church proper.

To pious Christians, the Tomb itself, which is the fourteenth and final station of the "Way of the Cross," represents the climax of their pilgrimage; a fulfillment of their religious longings to share in the Passion, Death and, ultimately, the Resurrection, of their Lord and Saviour.

The Tomb of Jesus, within the Holy Sepulchre. A marble slab raised above the floor level marks the place believed to be the actual rock which, from Friday sunset until sunrise on Sunday, served as the earthly funeral bed of Jesus.

Part Two: Judaism in the Holy Land

THE SECOND TEMPLE

The covenant God made with Israel pre-occupied the Prophets more than anything else. Indeed, it is central to everything they taught about God and man. Israel, they believed, was God's "light unto the nations." From Zion, God's peace, love and justice will descend upon the whole world.

These hopeful prophetic teachings continued to sustain the people when the Northern Kingdom of Israel fell in 722 B.C., and later, in 586, when Jerusalem and the Kingdom of Judah were conquered by the Babylonians. They took their law and love of God with them into exile, and in Babylonia they sang of Zion and remembered the vision of their Prophets. Thus after long years of exile, when the first wave of the people of Judah returned to Jerusalem in 538 B.C. under Ezra the Scribe, they were eager to hear the word of God spoken once more in Zion.

Nevertheless it was many years before the Second Temple, very much poorer than the First, was dedicated. Most historians believe that it took some seventeen years to build and that Zerubbabel did not complete the work until some time between 520 and 515 B.C. And even then, the Temple and the city itself were left unfortified and unprotected, at the mercy of enemies for over half a century. Not until 445 B.C., when Nehemiah was sent as governor, were the walls of the city rebuilt, although within a smaller area than the city's previous precincts. The building and supervision of the walls' construction were organized under the most trying security conditions.

The Second Temple, however, stood even longer than Solomon's first sanctuary. It remained for some five hundred years, until the time of Herod, who refashioned it into a place of great magnificence. No longer would the Temple be defiled by the introduction of pagan cults and rites; now, at last, it would become the single centre of adoration of the one and only God. The Holy of Holies remained empty, since the Ark with the Tablets of the Covenant had disappeared. But a new and powerful force was entering the religious life of the people. No longer did Judaism depend upon worship in the sanctuary, but now it saw the word of the Lord as Torah — divine teaching, eternal, transcendent, universal.

This must have been one of the influences of the Babylonian exile. Now the word at Sinai, if reverently recorded and made into a Sacred Scripture, could be studied and taught anywhere, by Israel itself or by those influenced by Israel. It was at this point in the history of Israel, during the lifetime of Ezra the Scribe, that the Five Books of Moses were edited.

It was later that these books, known also by their Greek name as the Pentateuch, were joined to the Former Prophets (books of history which chronicle the conquest of Canaan to the fall of Jerusalem) and then to the Later Prophets (the twelve "Minor Prophets" and the three "Major Prophets"). By 100 A.D., the third section, "The Writings," reached its present form, to complete the whole of the Hebrew Bible, or the Old Testament, as Christians would later come to call the sacred literature of the Hebrews.

THE HASMONEANS

Alexander the Great defeated the Persian empire in 332 B.C., and Jerusalem came under the sway of the Greeks, who did not physically oppress the Jews, but whose pagan style threatened the growth and free development of monotheistic Judaism. During the next few centuries, Palestine became a plaything in the hands of the contending parts of the Greek world, the Ptolemies of Egypt and the Seleucids of Syria. Some years later the Syrian king, Antiochus IV – also known as Epiphanus, or "God made manifest" – built a Greek gymnasium in Jerusalem and established the Akra, or fortress, in order to show his might. Then he proceeded to terrorize the inhabitants of Jerusalem by introducing a statue of Zeus in the Temple and abolishing the worship of Yahweh, the God of Israel.

But in 168 B.C., from the hill country of Judaea, in the town of Modin, a resistance movement formed around the Hasmonean priestly family of Mattathias and his sons. The most daring of these was Judah, called the Maccabee, or "Hammer," who gave his name to the new movement. Under his leadership the Temple was purified and returned to Jewish worship. Some years later, Simon, and then his son, John Hyrcanus of the Hasmonean family, re-established the Jewish kingdom, and become the heads of a new dynasty. But their claim upon the high priesthood and the royal office had no status in Jewish history, and their hold upon the people began to wane.

A number of Jewish sects were appearing on the scene, and the Hasmoneans had to seek an alliance with one or another. The major group was the Sadducees, whose adherents came from the priestly sector of the population and from the wealthy aristocrats whose conservative views had been shaped by the priestly tradition. Ranged against these was another group, the Pharisees – meaning "separatists," thus dubbed by the Sadducees – who wished to suggest that these Jews who questioned their priestly rule were, in fact, separating themselves from the people. But the Pharisees, recruited from the lower social and economic classes, would one day become the leaders of the people. Indeed, their leadership was not based upon the power of the court, or of the Temple priesthood. They were teachers or rabbis, whose mastery of the Torah, as learned students of the tradition, gave them a new authority for the day when the Temple would no longer stand.

There were still others who sought to "adjust" Judaism quite differently – by moving to the solitude of the desert, where Israel could recapture the simpler days of the Exodus. These were the Essenes, who probably formed monastic communities in several desert regions. Indeed, some scholars believe that the Qumran community, adjacent to the caves where the Dead Sea Scrolls were discovered, may have been an Essene outpost in the Judaean wilderness.

HEROD

Already on the horizon was the hulking power of Rome, and soon the star of the Hasmoneans would be on the decline. By the year 37 B.C., Herod, not even a Jew but an Idumean, traditionally an enemy of the Jews, became King, with the agreement and by the support of Rome. Until he died in 4 B.C., he reigned unchallenged over Palestine.

As a foreign king, hated and distrusted by his subjects, Herod was accepted grudgingly; his might was overwhelming and fearsome. When away from Jerusalem, he lived like a Greek monarch, and in the City of David itself he showed precious little respect for the feelings of the Jews. He built a theatre, hippodrome, amphitheatre — all pagan institutions. But in order to win their favour, he sought to conciliate his Jewish subjects by undertaking a sumptuous reconstruction of the Temple. This great, heroic work was begun in the year 20 B.C., and was not completed – some believe – until almost eighty-five years later – in 64 A.D., only six years before its destruction by the Romans!

To have some idea of the scope and size of the undertaking, all one needs to do is look at the enormous slabs of the so-called Wailing Wall, the outer Western Wall of Herod's Temple which still stands, placed together without cement. The walls served as a vast enclosure, requiring eight different entrance gates with two courts – the Court of the Gentiles, to which pagans were admitted, and an interior court for the Jews. Indeed, two inscriptions forbidding access to the Jewish court to gentiles or pagans have been discovered.

A third court, reserved for priests and levites, was placed in front of the Temple itself, which stood on a raised platform with fourteen steps leading up to it. Herod's Temple followed the design of Solomon's, but it was on a much grander scale, and with decorations as lavish as its architecture was heroic. The symbol of Israel, in the form of a vine of gold, was placed at its top, and golden needles spiked the roof in order to prevent birds from tainting it.

But despite all of its glories, the Temple was destined to be superseded in actual daily religious habit by a new and different institution, the synagogue. The synagogue came into being as a place of prayer and study, and it influenced not only the development of Judaism but also the growth of Christianity and Islam. When the Temple fell to the Romans in 70 A.D., much was lost, but Judaism lived on – not only in the new Roman exile, but also in the Holy Land.

LIFE BEYOND

One of the strong weapons in the spiritual arsenal of the Pharisee-Rabbis was the new emphasis they now placed upon the individual. In contrast to the Sadducee-Priests, whose principal concerns were centred in the Temple cult, the Pharisees gave new meaning to personal ethics, highlighted the role of prayer against cultic sacrifice, and assigned to each person in Israel a priestly function. It was this preoccupation with the person, and not only with the group, that brought about the development by the Rabbis of a new religious doctrine: retribution in a future world.

The Sadducees were opposed to this view, because they claimed that it was unbiblical, not specifically recorded in the written Torah. But the Pharisees were trying to solve that vexing problem of why the righteous suffer and the wicked prosper. They therefore took over the teaching of the Prophets concerning the End of Days – a teaching about the final redemption that was to come to Israel and the world – and applied it to the life and death of the individual person.

In biblical Judaism, death was a shadowy affair. The souls of the dead went to a nether world, which somehow was outside the realm of God's justice. The Pharisee-Rabbis changed this. They taught that the body dies but that the soul is immortal. God's justice, they thus made clear, extends beyond life. The souls of the righteous are with God, as the reward for their good deeds in life.

Out of concern for the individual and the meaning of his life, the Rabbis created this idea of "other-worldliness." Yet, they never allowed the Jews to neglect "this-worldliness." They never rejected this world in their acceptance of another world. In order to inherit the world to come, the Rabbis taught, one must live according to God's word, on earth.

To give effect to their views, they described the time to come in such allegorical terms as these: On the Day of Resurrection all will be gathered together on the Mount of Olives; the seat of judgment will be on Mount Moriah which is opposite. Over the Valley of Jehoshaphat between the two mountains, two bridges will appear, over which the resurrected ones will cross to their judgment, one of paper, for the Jews; the other, massive and strong, made of iron. All the heathen will cross over the iron bridge which will collapse under them. All the Jews will pass over the bridge of paper in peace and safety and will inherit eternal life.

On the slopes of the Mount of Olives, facing the ancient Temple Mount, the oldest, largest, and most sacred Jewish cemetery in the world patiently awaits this Day of Resurrection.

PIETISTS AND ZEALOTS

There were those among the Pharisees who were animated by mystical longings for personal communion with God, and by passionate, pious hopes for the end of history and the immediate coming of the Kingdom not of this world. The Jewish historian, Flavius Josephus, describes one group of break-away Pharisees, the Essenes, depicting their communal life in the desert as they wait for the destruction of Rome and the beginning of the End of Days.

Other groups have only recently come to light, and they may, indeed, be the Essenes themselves. These are the Dead Sea sects, particularly the Qumran community whose religious community was unearthed after the discovery of the Dead Sea Scrolls. They, too, had broken off from the Pharisees, and concentrated their prayers and hopes on the Kingdom of God, which they felt was at hand.

But there were other Jews, whose activism against the Roman powers gave their religious fervour a completely different colouration. Overlooking the Dead Sea, in the Judaean desert rock-fortress of Masada, on the site where Herod the Great had erected some of his most daring buildings, there was to be enacted one of the most dramatic episodes in religious history. On this immense rock, rising above the western shore of the Dead Sea, some twenty miles north of Sodom, hundreds of Jewish zealots preferred to kill themselves rather than surrender to the imperial tyranny of pagan Rome.

When the Zealots of Masada went down before the Roman Tenth Legion in 73 A.D., their leader, Eleazar ben Yair summoned them on the night before their mass suicide. His words, recorded for posterity by Flavius Josephus, possibly constitute one of the most dramatic addresses in recorded history:

"All men are equally destined to death; and the same fate attends the coward as the brave. Can we think of submitting to the indignity of slavery? Can we behold our wives dishonoured and our children enslaved? Let us die free men, gloriously surrounded by our wives and children. Eternal renown shall be ours by snatching the prize from the hands of our enemies, and leaving them nothing to triumph over but the bodies of those who dared to be their own executioners."

Thus, to the very end, the Zealots defied the power of Rome. Their brave example lived on in the hearts of the Jews who survived them. Theirs was a piety of another kind, reminiscent of the ringing watchword of later centuries: "Rebellion to tyrants is obedience to God."

THE SYNAGOGUE

When modern Jews refer to their synagogues as temples they are committing an historical error. There is only one Temple in Jewish life, the Temple on Mount Zion. That Temple – first built by Solomon, but destroyed by Nebuchadnezzar in 586 B.C.; then rebuilt as the Second Temple, and later reconstructed by Herod; only to be finally destroyed by the Romans in 70 A.D. – had a biblical mandate. How it came to be built, maintained, and operated was fully described in the Bible. A full set of laws and practices was minutely formulated to govern the institution of the Temple, the plan and purpose of which were divinely preconceived. Each day, morning and afternoon, there were sacrifices on the altar. Pilgrims from all over the land thronged to it, especially during the three harvest festivals of spring, summer, and fall. The building itself

– particularly Herod's Temple – was elaborately and splendidly built, and its physical majesty was matched by the rich aura of the religious service conducted by the priests and the levitical choirs and orchestra, whose tones overflowed into the chambers and the outer courts.

In contrast to the Temple, the synagogue had a much humbler origin. It came upon the scene as a human accommodation to the circumstances of history some time after the first Temple had been destroyed. When the exiles returned to their land to build the Second Temple, they carried attachments to this new and popular form of religious expression. From this time forward, despite the existence of the Temple, emphasis began to shift, although almost imperceptibly at first, from the sanctity of the priests to the sanctity of the people, from the place of worship to the gathering of worshippers. The people became a holy congregation.

While the synagogue substituted prayer for Temple sacrifice – thus it had no altar – it became even more than a House of Prayer. Under the influence of the Rabbis it was made into a House of Study, a popular school of higher spiritual learning for adults. The reading and teaching of Scripture became a central, characteristic feature of Jewish public worship. The synagogue was also a public House of Assembly – such is the meaning of the Greek word synagogue – in which the community forgathered; its courts of law were convened there; strangers were made welcome and given lodging; and the poor were invited to receive alms.

The introduction of this radically new type of public religious institution upon the scene constituted a far-reaching departure not only in Judaism but in the very annals of religion. Clearly, the synagogue played an important role in shaping the future life and style of both the church and the mosque.

IN GALILEE

In 132 A.D., under the generalship of Bar Kochba, the final insurrection against Rome began. For three long years the Jewish forces held out in a bitter campaign, but were finally crushed by Hadrian's forces in 135. After this disastrous defeat, many Jews left Judaea to settle in Galilee, which soon became the seat of the Sanhedrin, the Supreme Court of Rabbis, and the new centre of religious and national life. By the close of the second and during the third century, contact between Jews and Romans was friendly, with the result that the economic condition of the country improved greatly. Throughout the Galilee district, prosperous towns and villages were now erecting fine synagogues, the remnants of which archaeologists have been constantly unearthing, some of which form the distinctive "Galilean Style" of the time.

An important feature of the Galilean synagogue was its orientation. By definition, "orientation" means "to face east," which is the traditional style of synagogues throughout the world, in supreme tribute to the important place of Jerusalem in the history and hopes of Judaism. But in the Holy Land itself, the Galilean synagogues faced south, in the direction of Jerusalem. Similarly, synagogues situated south of Jerusalem

faced north, while those in Transjordan "oriented" westward.

The decoration of the synagogues of the Holy Land during the Roman and Byzantine periods constitutes a most enigmatic and challenging question. To be sure, many of the motifs comprise geometrical and floral designs – leaves, fruits, and the vine, symbolizing the fertility of the Land. In addition, Jewish religious symbols abounded: the *menorah* or seven-branched candelabrum; the *lulav* or palm-branch, and *etrog* or citron used in the synagogue on the seven-day Feast of Tabernacles; the *shofar* or ram's horn, and others. But beyond these, the figurative imagery displayed prominently in many of these synagogues is most enigmatic, in the light of the strict biblical injunction of the second commandment, "you shall not make yourself a graven image, or any likeness of anything that is in heaven above, or that is in the earth beneath, or that is in the water under the earth; you shall not bow down to them or serve them. . . ." (Exodus 20:4-5)

Indeed, archaeologists have been shocking most traditional theologians. Their discoveries have revealed the astonishing fact that, contrary to previous assumptions, the Jews in Roman and Byzantine times avoided neither the plastic nor the pictorial arts. In searching the written sources there is evidence of the leniency of some Talmudic Rabbis, great scholars, who interpreted the Second Commandment liberally: they were willing to permit pictorial representation of religious themes, influenced as they were by the Greek spirit of the times, contenting themselves with a strong warning that the images themselves must neither be nor become objects of worship. Thus it was that the synagogues of the Holy Land soon became the centre of a new Jewish art which enjoyed great popularity among the people. The Bible stories came to be depicted figuratively within the synagogue, and the arts were used as instruments for both aesthetic and educational effects.

TIBERIAS AND SAFAD

The power of Rome was vast and insistent. In Galilee, the small Jewish congregations continued to subsist throughout the early Christian centuries, but the larger and more-developed Jewish communities were to be found in the exile, the cities of Babylonia. It was there that the vaunted Babylonian Talmud was developed and there that Jewish life and learning flourished. But by the ninth century, Tiberias on the Sea of Galilee and towns nearby became seats of new learning. Members of the Tiberias academy, the Masoretes as they were called, were especially concerned with correcting and copying precisely the biblical text itself, and they developed what has been called after them "the Masoretic tradition." To them, more than to all others, history owes the preservation of an authentic and properly transmitted text of the Old Testament.

Scattered Jews remained in the land all these years, but several centuries were to elapse before the Holy Land would again figure prominently in actual Jewish resettlement. Between 1209 and 1211, there was a considerable immigration. Over three hundred Rabbis of France and England went up to Jerusalem as new settlers of the country. Within a generation, in 1258, another wave followed, led by Rabbi Yehiel of Paris, who founded the Talmudical Academy of Paris in the coastal city of Acre. Then, in 1267, the great Rabbi of Spain, Nahmanides, settled in the

Holy Land. Moved by the failure of the Crusades, other Jews began to arrive toward the close of the thirteenth century.

It took a combination of factors at the opening of the sixteenth century to make possible large-scale Jewish return to the land. In 1492, in Spain, the richest and most numerous Jewish community in Europe was offered a choice: either convert to Christianity or emigrate. The same fate came upon Portuguese Jewry six years later. Then, in 1517, Selim I, the Ottoman Turkish Sultan, added Syria, Egypt, and Arabia to his empire. This gave beleaguered Iberian Jewry an opportunity to settle in Palestine, for the Sultan encouraged settlement. Great numbers of Jews took advantage of his tolerant attitude and a major immigration began.

It was principally to a Galilean town, unknown to biblical students, that most of them came. In the Galilean mountains, perched some 2,700 feet above sea level, a new capital town was in the making, the beautiful town of Safad. Four thousand feet below lies the Sea of Galilee, which can be seen from its outskirts. To the west is the land's highest mountain, Jebel Jarmak, or Mount Meron, enshrining the tombs of gentle Rabbi Hillel and his disciples and other Rabbis.

This part of Galilee seemed always to have a special attraction for pietists and mystics. Yet it was not until the early sixteenth century that the city became the centre not only of the Jews of the Holy Land but also of Jews around the world. This was made a reality not only because of the large number of scholars, saints, and mystics who came but also because of the region's relative security atop the mountains. Safad had a strategic position close by the caravan route to Acre, leading to

Damascus. Before long, the manufacture of woollen goods, which were sold in the markets of Damascus, was successfully developed in Safad.

Nevertheless, the major attraction of Safad to most of the Jewish mystics who arrived during the sixteenth century was neither its commerce nor its scenic beauty. It was essentially its proximity to nearby Mount Meron, the burial place of Rabbi Simon bar Yohai, reputed author of the basic book of Cabbalism, *The Zohar*, or the Book of Splendour, which served as the real magnet. After the expulsion from Spain, *The Zohar*, a book of mystical speculation, achieved a rank of significance among Jews, second only to the Bible and the Talmud. The dark hour of Spain was now seen as but a forerunner to a new dawn and the coming of the Messiah. It was in Galilee, but particularly in Safad, that a new fervour and excitement, the product of mystical and Messianic speculations, took hold of the imagination and spread across the Jewish world.

THE NEW DAWNING

During the next centuries, Jews of the Diaspora – those who lived outside the Holy Land – would go up to the Holy Land in their declining years with the expressed desire to die there. It was their hope to be interred in its sacred soil, in anticipation of their resurrection which, they believed, would follow the arrival of Messianic days. The unique relationship of the land of Israel to the religion of Israel is a constant element in Jewish history. The Promised Land was more than a national goal; it was a concrete reality expressing the covenant God made with Abraham and his seed after him.

But it also was the very stage for a system of biblical laws – agricultural and labour legislation – that gave meaning and focus to the ethical character of Judaism. Rooted in the very soil of Israel are biblical laws dealing with social justice, the prevention of poverty, and the public concern due the orphan, the widow, and the dispossessed. Although the Jews were exiled and forcibly separated from the Holy Land for centuries, the prayers of synagogues everywhere continued to echo the people's nostalgia for the soil and the skies, the rain and the dew, the fruit and the trees of the land.

While it was given a major prod and stimulation by the rising tide of national awakening which came upon the world in the nineteenth century, the Jewish return to the land, which began in earnest in the middle of that century, stemmed principally from older religious teachings. And even those Jews who did not define themselves primarily in religious terms, but saw themselves rather as nationalists intent upon regaining their ancient homeland, could not move very far without buttressing their thought with the Bible.

Since 1881, following persecution of the Jews in Eastern Europe, large numbers settled on the land. Today, more than two decades after their land has been incorporated into the body politic of the United Nations as the sovereign State of Israel, more than two and a half million Jewish citizens live on the soil made holy by its religious history. The ancient language of the Prophets, Hebrew, has been revivified, and is again the language of the land. Old villages, towns, valleys, and mountains have sprung to life again after sleeping away the centuries. The old has become new, and the new has become sacred.

Herod's Palace as seen in the reconstructed model of the old city of Jerusalem at the Holyland Hotel.

Looking at the Jewish cemetery on the Mount of Olives from the Valley of Jehoshaphat below. In Hebrew, the name Jehoshaphat means "God shall judge."
Zechariah had thought of the slopes of the Mount of Olives as the scene of God's future judgment of mankind. The Prophet Joel, foreseeing the time of Jerusalem's fall, had also prophesied the future judgment. It was thus regarded as desirable, among Jews, to be buried as close as possible to this spot in view of the final Resurrection.
In the foreground is the so-called "Tomb of Absalom," probably from the third century B.C. In the centre, from the same period, is a monument for the priestly House of Hezir. Christian tradition believes that in this grotto James was arrested, which accounts for its Christian name, the Grotto of St. James. To the right, from the same period, is another tomb, "The Tomb of Zechariah."

The catacombs of Beth She'arim.
Most frequent symbols in the catacombs are the seven-branched candelabrum, the ram's horn, and the citron and palm branch used at the Feast of Tabernacles.
There are also pictorializations of a Roman legionary and gladiators, and Biblical episodes such as Noah's Ark and Daniel in the lion's den.
So far over 300 different burial inscriptions have been found.

A *sarcophagus* at the catacombs of Beth She'arim, which was opened by grave-robbers seeking precious objects.

101

On the shores of the Dead Sea at Qumran, some miles from Jericho, a small group of pietistic Pharisees split away from their Jerusalem centre and established a commune for themselves. Some scholars believe that these were, in fact, the Essenes.

These are the people who produced the world-renowned Dead Sea Scrolls. Recent excavations have unearthed the remains of the structures they built. Turning their backs on the city, it was the Desert of Judaea which called forth their deepest spiritual longings. They believed that trade was evil. They condemned slavery, abstained from taking oaths, and sought a life of ritual and ethical purity in their desert village. Many of the teachings of the Qumran community clearly had important influences on the life and style of John the Baptist, and thus, they may be seen as a bridge group between the faith of Judaism and the early beginnings of Christianity.

The Isaiah Scroll, one of the most significant of the Dead Sea Scrolls, dominates the interior of the "Shrine of the Book" built by the Israel Museum in Jerusalem. The unique display case, seen here, is in the shape of a scroll.

Masada, in the Wilderness of Judaea, near the Dead Sea: An aerial view from the north showing the three terraces of Herod's hanging palace, built on the Rock of Masada. On the precipice of the lower terrace the remains of a huge supporting wall are still visible. It is probable that Herod built this palace-villa on an isolated, difficult part of Masada because of its natural defence advantage, its proximity to cisterns, and its shelters from sun and wind.

Excavations have also brought to light the remains of the Zealots – about a thousand Jews who lived atop Masada after the fall of Jerusalem in 70 A.D. and who, for three years thereafter, held out against the Tenth Roman Legion. When they could no longer withstand the Romans, rather than surrender they took their own lives as an act of national defiance.

A main feature of the Galilean synagogue of the first centuries was its elaborate façade. The front wall usually had a large middle portal, and there were two smaller side doors, one leading into a nave, the other, down the aisle. Since Galilean synagogues were located in the north of the country, all were "oriented" toward Jerusalem, facing south.

Near the border with Lebanon is Bar'am, seen here, which presents the best-preserved façade of the early Galilean synagogues. Its central doorway was most elaborate – its lintel was decorated with the figures of two Victories holding a wreath. Yet, because of the greater orthodoxy and iconoclastic tendencies of later centuries, these decorations can be seen to have been painstakingly erased.

Near the Synagogue at Meron is the Tomb of Rabbi Simon bar Yohai, a second-century Rabbi who lived under Roman rule, and who is considered to be the father of Jewish mysticism and the author of the major Cabbalistic work, *The Zohar*.

The Cabbalists of Safad, the world centre of mystical speculation among Jews in the Middle Ages, make regular pilgrimages to Rabbi Simon's grave, particularly on *Lag B'Omer*, which occurs several weeks after Passover. On that night, they remove a Scroll of the Torah from a Safad synagogue, march with it in procession the five miles to his Tomb, where they dance with it until dawn. Prayers are recited daily before the tomb without interruption.

Inside the Tomb of Rabbi Simon bar Yohai, devout worshippers, mostly Oriental Jews, recite prayers. The tomb of Rabbi Simon's son Eliezer is also found inside the building.

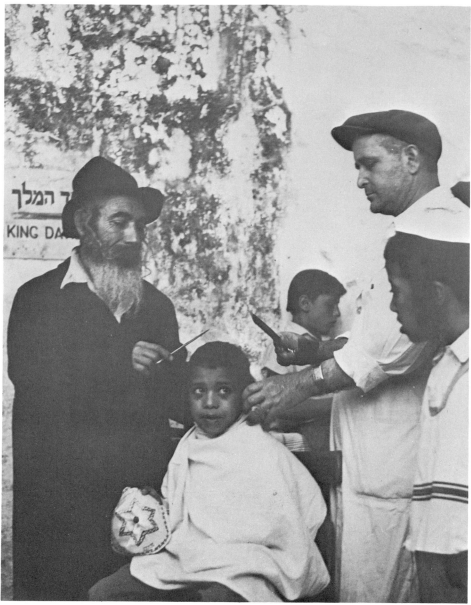

The holiday of *Lag B'Omer* has special customs associated with it. Bonfires are lit throughout the countryside to commemorate the day, the scholar's holiday. At Meron, adult pranksters play games and cavort. And this day, the thirty-third following Passover, is also set aside for first haircuts for the young children of religious parents. Adjacent to King David's Tomb on Jerusalem's Mount Zion, young lads are shorn on *Lag B'Omer.*

From the sixteenth century, mountainous Safad attracted pious Jewish scholars and mystics, principally from among those who were forced to leave Inquisitorial Spain. That century became the golden age of Safad.
The old city hangs on the mountainside, and from its winding and twisting alleys, medieval synagogues may still be visited.

A cobble-stoned alley in hilly Safad. The city still has many pious Jews, who look as if the sixteenth century never passed away, and for whom time seems to stand still.

The interior of the Sephardic Synagogue in Safad showing the Torah Ark with its ornate and colourful marble columns. The synagogue was built in honour of the great Cabbalistic teacher, Rabbi Isaac Luria, called "The Lion," or *Ari*.

The entrance to the "Ari" Synagogue.

111

Opposite page.
Many of the old traditions are coming back to life in the contemporary Judaism now lived by more than two and a half million Jewish citizens of the State of Israel. Here, an improvised Torah canopy set up on the site of the ancient synagogue ruin atop Masada. A group of young Israelis from an agricultural settlement accompany their thirteen-year-old friend to this ancient place to participate in the celebration of his religious coming-of-age, the Bar-Mitzvah ceremony.

This page.
Old, traditional habits of prayer persist, even in new and unusual settings. Garbed in prayer shawls, young members of an Israeli army unit celebrate the Sabbath in the field.

A wedding at Kibbutz Yad
Mordechai, south of the
city of Ashkelon, near the
Gaza Strip.
A Rabbi from the nearby city
brings his wedding canopy
to the great outdoors of the
kibbutz to perform the
marriage under the stars.

Seven weeks following Passover, the Festival of
Shavuot – the Feast of
Weeks – is celebrated.
In the cities, synagogue
services recall that it is
also the Festival of First
Fruits. But at the kibbutz,
the festival is celebrated
naturally, in song and in dance,
in gratitude for the harvest.
Here "Kibbutzniks" at Gan
Shmuel celebrate the old
holiday in spirited, new
ways.

Opposite page left. The Great Synagogue of Tel Aviv, on Allenby Road.

Opposite page right. A small synagogue in Netanya, an Israeli coastal resort town. Throughout Israel, there are some 6,000 synagogues serving a population of 2½ million Jews. Jews from the two major religious traditions dwell side by side: the *Sephardim*, who stem from Mediterranean and Near Eastern lands, and the *Ashkenazim*, who represent the Jewish communities which came to Israel from European lands.

At the head of Israel's Rabbinate are two Chief Rabbis, one for each of these major communities. Seen this page left are the Chief Rabbis: Ashkenazi Rabbi Unterman with the silk hat; Sephardi Rabbi Nissim with the turban.

This page right we see *Heichal Shlomo* – the seat of the Chief Rabbinate of Israel in Jerusalem. Under Israeli law, every religious community – Christian, Muslim, Druze, as well as Jewish – may govern its own communicants under its own religious law, in religious courts of its own, in matters dealing with personal status.

On special occasions, religious pilgrims are summoned by blasts on the ram's horn from atop Mount Zion in Jerusalem.

For almost twenty years, from 1948 until 1967, Jews had no access to the Western Wall, and thus, Mount Zion, the holy place nearest the Wall, became the major scene of special devotions in honour of the ancient Temple.

Sephardic Jews stand on Mount Zion, calling the faithful to make a pilgrimage from the lower city to the heights of Zion. Seen here are the long and curled ram's horns – the *shofar* – in the style of Near-Eastern Jewish custom. The men wear the traditional woolen *tallit*, or prayer-shawl.

Today the Western Wall, which is dominated by the Dome of the Rock, has become a major national shrine of the people of Israel. Literally thousands come to it, day and night, and prayer services are held almost continually.

For Jews everywhere the Wall has become a symbol of the rebirth of Zion, and the hope that the City of David, from whence the word once came forth to the whole world, may again become a light unto the nations and serve man's highest hopes.

"For my house shall be called a House of Prayer for all peoples."

An Israeli soldier praying at the Western Wall, or so-called Wailing Wall, shortly after the Israeli Army, in June 1967, captured the Old City of Jerusalem. The Western Wall, built by Herod the Great as the outer, exterior perimeter of the Temple Mount, consists of typically massive Herodian-style stones. For centuries, since the fall of the Temple to the Romans, pious Jews have come to the Wall to lament the loss of Zion and the people's exile. Hence, Christians and Muslims called it the Wailing Wall.

Part Three: Christianity in the Holy Land

THE SPREAD OF CHRISTIANITY

When the Temple fell in the year 70 A.D., Palestine ceased to have a history of its own. For many centuries thereafter, interest in the country was to be maintained largely by outsiders – by peoples from different parts of the world who sought to conquer the land. Thus the growth and development of the country must be sought in forces and factors that had their motivations and origins elsewhere. Palestine, as the object of others' desires, religious or otherwise, could barely have a life of its own for centuries to come.

It was entirely natural that, with the spread of Christianity throughout the Roman Empire, a new and growing interest in the land of Jesus would be sparked. Beginning with the closing decades of the fourth century, with the accession of Theodosius the Great as Emperor, an epoch of great Christian growth was ushered into the Holy Land. Theodosius proclaimed the primacy of the Christian faith within his empire in 380, and slowly but surely the majority of those who were to live in the Holy Land in the next several centuries were to be converted to the Christian faith. Soon enough the last traces of Roman paganism were to be torn down, and the entire country would be transformed into a Christian patrimony.

The Holy Land was greatly enhanced, for it benefited materially from the new interest of world Christendom in the biblical sites and from a growing preoccupation with the building of monuments to mark places made sacred by mention in the Old and New Testaments. Jerusalem benefited most, and it was to become the focal point of monument-building. In 451, at the Church Council of Chalcedon, the Bishop of Jerusalem, until that time merely a suffragan to the Metropolitan of Caesarea in the north, was raised to the high and significant rank of Patriarch of Jerusalem. And this Patriarchate was placed at the head of all other regions of Palestine, with some seventy bishops subordinate to its rule.

THE GREEK ORTHODOX PATRIARCHATE

The present Greek Orthodox Patriarch of Jerusalem, His Beatitude, Kyr Benedictos I, is the ninety-fifth in succession since that day in 451 when the Council of Chalcedon proclaimed Bishop Juvenal first Patriarch of Jerusalem. In the centuries immediately following the inauguration of the Patriarchate, the region developed greatly, favoured as it was by the Byzantine emperors, and it flourished as the centre of pilgrimages from all parts of the Christian world. Its chief function, however, was to guard and preserve the holy places for the Christian world.

In 638, the powers of the Patriarch were severely curtailed, as a result of the Muslim conquest of Jerusalem. Caliph Omar ibn el Khattab, the second Caliph, took the Holy City, and Patriarch Sophronius was subordinated to him. The Caliph granted him an *ahtnamé*, in which the rights and the privileges of the Patriarch of Jerusalem were guaranteed. In accordance with this undertaking, the Muslims recognized the Patriarch as the owner of all the Holy Shrines inside and outside of Jerusalem and of the monasteries and churches throughout the land. He was recognized also as the Ethnarch and the spiritual leader of the Greek Orthodox inhabitants of the Holy Land, as well as the leader of the non-Greek Christians living within the limits of his Patriarchal See.

Over the centuries considerable friction developed between the three major Christian interests in the Holy Land – the Greek Orthodox, the Latins (as the Roman Catholics are known to this day in the Middle East), and the Armenian Christians. To preserve order and maintain the dignity of the relationships among these groups, as well as other religious interests in the Holy Land, a document known as "The Status Quo" was drawn up in the eighteenth century. It was adopted by the Conference of Paris in 1856, and reconfirmed by the Treaty of Berlin in 1878. Indeed, twice in the twentieth century, both by the League of Nations and the United Nations, the principle of "the status quo" was readopted: Everything the Greeks, the Latins, and the Armenians held either in common or in sole possession should forever remain as before.

The Greek Orthodox Patriarchate, in addition to the role it plays at these Holy Places, also possesses a large number of historic churches, monasteries, and convents, both in Jerusalem and throughout the country. In addition, it maintains over eighty churches, and some forty-five primary and secondary community schools of a religious character, all through the Holy Land.

The Patriarchate is considered by the Greek Church as autocephalic. While federated to the Greek Orthodox community throughout the world, it is independent of any outside authority. It is governed solely by the Patriarch of Jerusalem, with the assistance of a Holy Synod, consisting of fourteen priests. An overall Brotherhood of some hundred monks constitutes the general body, whose principal concern remains the care and preservation of the holy places, and the reception and instruction of Christian pilgrims to the land.

THE LATIN PATRIARCHATE

The Roman Catholic or Latin Patriarchate of Jerusalem was not founded until 1099, following the conquest of the city by the first Crusaders. In the temporary absence of a Greek Orthodox Patriarch – the last one, Simeon, had recently died in Cyprus, where he had gone seeking refuge from the Muslims – the Crusaders installed their own Patriarch. During the next eighty-eight years, during which the Latin Kingdom of the Crusaders was sovereign in Jerusalem, the Greek Orthodox Patriarchs of Jerusalem were constrained to reside and function in Constantinople, not in Jerusalem.

The Latin Patriarchate in Jerusalem never did rival the power and prestige of the Greek Orthodox Patriarchate, yet it soon proceeded to cover its diocese with several remarkable monuments, some of which – parts of the Holy Sepulchre, the Tomb of the Virgin, the churches of St. Anne, Abu-Ghosh, and others – have survived to this day. But when the Latin Kingdom of the Crusaders fell to Saladin in 1187, the Patriarchs of Jerusalem reigned in Acre until it too fell in 1291. Within a few years the Patriarchate itself was disbanded, and the Franciscan Fathers took over the Latin charge in Jerusalem. The Franciscans came to be regarded as the "Custos of the Holy Land," the custodians on behalf of the Roman Catholics of the holy places in the Holy Land.

It was not until 1847 that the institution of the Latin Patriarchate of Jerusalem was restored. Since then it has been assisted by many religious institutions. First and foremost is the Franciscan Custody of the Holy Land, the oldest Catholic institution in the country, the largest in size, and the most important in scope and significance. For many centuries now it has continually ministered to most of the important Christian sanctuaries, including the Holy Sepulchre in Jerusalem, and the Church of the Nativity in Bethlehem, which it shares jointly with the Greeks and the Armenians. Moreover, the Franciscans, in 1924, established the Biblical Institute of Higher Studies in Jerusalem, which has achieved universal acclaim as a school of religious learning.

Many other Catholic orders of nuns, priests, and monks are entrusted with various holy structures. The Carmelites, who arrived in the Holy Land in 1631, are in charge of the sanctuaries of Mount Carmel, as well as the Latin Parish of the Haifa area. The Dominicans have their world-renowned Ecole Biblique in Jerusalem; the Benedictines have the Abbey of the Dormition on Mount Zion; the Trappists control the Abbey of Latrun; the Assumptionists, dedicated to encouraging Catholic pilgrims to the Holy Land, have a number of important churches in their charge, including St. Peter's in Gallicantu on Mount Zion.

Catholics of the Byzantine rite in the Holy Land – Eastern Christians who are in communion with Rome, principally Arab converts to Christianity – have their own Patriarch, currently resident in Damascus. These people are known as Greek Catholics or Melkites, and while the majority live in the Arab villages of the Galilee, most of their clergy are trained in their Seminary at the beautiful Crusader Church of St. Anne, in the Old City of Jerusalem, which is directed by the White Fathers. In addition to the Greek Catholics, there are also smaller numbers of Maronites who live close to the Lebanon border, around Haifa and Nazareth and in the ancient Galilean village of Gush-Halav. The Maronites derive from Lebanon, trace their ancestry to ancient Phoenicia, and are called after St. Maron, a fifth-century Lebanese Christian.

In all, the Roman Catholics and those in communion with them have a long and continuous history in the Holy Land.

THE ARMENIAN PATRIARCHATE

The connections of Armenians to Palestine reach back to pre-Christian days. Indeed, the Tenth Roman Legion which conquered Jerusalem was mainly composed of Armenians from Melitene.

Christianity was brought to Armenia by the third century. The Church was founded by two of the Apostles of Jesus, Bartholomew and Thaddeus, who won over a good part of the Armenian people. In the year 301, Christianity became the national and state religion of Armenia, when King Tiridates the Great was baptized. Armenia was thus the first nation to become Christian, decades before the acceptance of Christianity by the Roman Empire. Armenian attachment to Jerusalem is of long standing too, and old traditions recall their community living and worshipping on the Mount of Olives as early as the third century.

The Greek Orthodox Patriarchate, the Latin Partriarchate, and the Armenian Patriarchate are the three main custodians of the Christian holy places. The Armenian Patriarchate enjoys the sole ownership, however, of the historic Cathedral of St. James, which stands on the site of the House of St. James the Less, Jerusalem's first Bishop. It is located in the Armenian quarter of the Old City of Jerusalem, which occupies almost one-sixth of the entire area within the city's walls. Organized as a monastic brotherhood, the Patriarchate is composed of nine Bishops, thirty-two Archimandrites, and seventy monks. The Patriarch is the spiritual leader of the Church, the president of all assemblies, and the governor of church properties, which, in addition to the Armenian quarter of Jerusalem, also include monasteries in Jaffa and Ramla, and a large monastery in Bethlehem near the Church of the Nativity. The General Assembly of all the members of the brotherhood elects the Patriarch and also establishes a Holy Synod to assist him in discharging his temporal and spiritual duties.

In addition to the Greek Orthodox, Latin, and Armenian Patriarchs, there are three other less-powerful and less-numerous Christian groups which have maintained continuous ties with Jerusalem for many centuries. The Jacobites, officially known as the Syrian Orthodox, have a bishopric in Jerusalem since 1140. The Copts, who maintain a convent beside the Holy Sepulchre Church, have been there since 1219. The Abyssinians, too, have several convents in the Holy Land, and for many centuries have maintained ties to Jerusalem. Indeed, according to them, the eldest of their Jerusalem monasteries, Deir es-Sultan, is located on the very site where the Queen of Sheba was said to have been domiciled in the city when she paid her historic visit to King Solomon.

BYZANTINE MONASTERIES

The Byzantine era, which stretches from the fourth to the seventh century, is the real Christian period in Palestine. Everywhere new shrines and sanctuaries came into being. The Christian villages of Galilee and Samaria, many of which still exist, originated in the Byzantine era, and archaeologists have shown how the more recent churches were erected on the foundations of earlier Byzantine structures. This fact, in particular, clearly reflects the vigorous strength inherent in early Christianity which did not merely conserve memorial sites but added to them.

The Byzantine era was marked by mass pilgrimages which have continued to this very day. The care and lodging of pilgrims demanded special hospices, and pilgrims' cemeteries had to be established, since some of the pilgrims wished to be buried close to the holy places.

A considerable share in the success of Christianity may be attributed to the institution of the monastery, which was introduced by Hilarion of Gaza from Egypt around 330. Thousands of monks came to live in numerous caves in the deep *wadis* of the Judaean desert, and these caves can still be admired. Monks settled in the abandoned Jewish fortresses of Masada and Herodium as well. There were twenty-four known monasteries on the Mount of Olives at that time, of which only one, Dominus Flevit, has been excavated.

Monasteries in the Holy Land dating from Byzantine times are located in some of the most inaccessible places in the country, often situated atop mountains or implanted within rocky gorges overlooking picturesque *wadis*, the dry river beds that stream with water only a few weeks each winter. They are not mere churches but fortress-like, self-sufficient communities, built to defy time and to outlast earthly kingdoms.

The monastic life, first begun in the fourth century in Egypt and Gaza, spread across the Judaean desert to the vicinity of the "two cities of the Incarnation," Jerusalem and Bethlehem. Hard by both cities were then and are today amazingly beautiful "hiding places," desert habitations most difficult to reach but from whose rooftops both the sprawling hills of Bethlehem and the green summit of the Mount of Olives may be easily seen.

St. Chariton of Anatolia was the first of many monks to settle in the Judaean wilderness. He originated the specifically Palestinian form of building: the *laura*, a row or cluster of solitary cells around a common centre, including a bakehouse, where the monks would assemble for Saturdays and Sundays, spending the rest of the week in solitude in their cells. Thus the *laura* suggests the unusual geographical character of the Byzantine wilderness monasteries – caves or cells opening out onto a path running along the side of a ravine. This conformed to the life-style of the ascetics. On Saturdays and Sunday mornings they brought together their produce, worshipped and ate together, transacted any necessary communal business, and then took back with them to their private cells enough bread, water, and materials for their handiwork during the course of the week ahead.

Monasteries of the *laura* type were for anchorites, monks who lived separately and apart. But in addition to these, there were also monasteries for cenobites, monks who shared a common life. These were established in cities and deserts both. There were also monasteries of a third kind which fostered such industries as the cultivation of the grape and the olive, and these welcomed travellers and traders from afar.

Most typical of the monasteries of the Holy Land are those perched somewhere in the middle of "nowhere," far away from civilization, resting in the eternal solitude of the wilderness. In such secluded monasteries, the sense of communion with the land and with the God who made himself known in the land must have been poignant and profound. One such retreat is the monastery near Jericho in Wadi Qelt.

The Monastery of Choziba, in Wadi Qelt, also known as the Greek Monastery of St. George, was built in the fifth century, as an anchorite *laura*. It "hangs" within sight of the Roman road to Jericho, on the steep north gorge of Wadi Qelt, the one tiny stream in all of this area of the Judaean wilderness. Along the sheer face of cliffs from behind, tortuous paths lead to anchorite cells.

For many centuries there was entertained a popular if erroneous tradition that the Monastery of Choziba was built on the actual bed of the Brook of Cherith. The brook is mentioned in the Old Testament and is where the Prophet Elijah was fed bread and flesh morning and evening by the ravens. Some modern scholars are of the opinion that this desolate, rocky area, pock-marked with caves, was first used by the Essenes, the Jewish sectarian ascetics of the first pre-Christian century.

In addition to their natural beauty and primitive architectural splendour, many of the Byzantine monasteries in the Holy Land have also been important repositories of great iconographic art. Extremely valuable biblical and early church manuscripts have been preserved in some of their libraries – in the very midst of the wilderness. By now, most of their noteworthy possessions have been removed to museums or church collections in the more "civilized" parts of the world. Yet visitors to these monasteries may still see many valuable works of great literary and religious significance.

Those Christians who secluded themselves in monasteries of the Judaean wilderness seem to have much in common with those Jews, some centuries earlier, who had turned their backs on cities and moved into the wilderness near the Dead Sea. From that community of Qumran have come the Dead Sea Scrolls. Perhaps these were written and preserved by the Essenes, who were described by Josephus and Pliny, or by other Jewish sectarians who were similarly oriented. The call of the desert was always strong, and it harks back to Elijah, to the Old Testament prophets of the eighth century, and, of course, to New Testament descriptions of the life of John the Baptist.

It is difficult to visualize the Holy Land without its ascetics and monastics. Indeed, in the biographies of Christian monks who lived in the Judaean wilderness more than a century ago it is not uncommon to find evidence that these monks believed themselves to be obedient to the call Abraham heard and obeyed by going to the same land almost two millenia earlier: "Go from your country and your kindred and your father's house to the land that I will show you." (Genesis 12:1)

THE CRUSADES

When Constantine published his edict in Caesarea in 324, which made Christianity the state religion of the Roman Empire, the Christian era commenced in the Holy Land. It lasted about three centuries, until Rome's implacable foes, the Persians, gained a short-lived dominion over the land. This concluded after fifteen years, with the victory of Byzantine Emperor Heraklios, who re-entered Jerusalem in 628 and with great pomp restored the Church of the Holy Sepulchre. But the Arabs were already on the march, knocking on the gates of the Holy Land. In 638, Jerusalem fell to the powerful Caliph Omar Ibn al-Khattab, and the Muslim period began.

Until the time the Crusader Kingdom was established in 1099, the Holy Land had known little peace. The Umayyad dynasty was followed by the advent of the Abbasids. Many churches were burned, Christians killed, and their religious freedom seriously proscribed. Nor were Christians greatly relieved when, in the tenth century, the land was conquered by the Fatimids, an Islamic dynasty of North Africa.

The Crusader Kingdom had a life of about two hundred years, from 1099 to 1187, and again, after a brief interregnum, from 1189 to 1291. To be sure, the motivations of the Crusaders who came to free the land from the grip of "the infidels" were most complex and diverse. Not all could possibly have been prompted solely by piety, nor was spirituality always at the root of their purpose. Yet there seems to be general agreement that the First Crusade was precipitated by concern throughout the Christian world over the violent conquest of the land by the Seljuk Turks.

Pope Urban II, of French origin, was probably the most fervent advocate of the First Crusade, with the result that numerous contingents of French Barons participated and lent to the Crusader rule in the Holy Land a particularly Gallic flavour. French knights were especially prominent in the military operation of the kingdom. But since the cost of maintaining the knights was so very high, in the course of time they were augmented by a new fighting arm, the various military orders.

These orders consisted of knights who were also ordained monks and who had taken the necessary vows to help the sick, to offer shelter and hospitality to pilgrims in the Holy Land. The most important was the Order of the Hospitallers, located near the Church of the Holy Sepulchre. Next in importance was the Order of the Templars, which derived its name from the fact that it was headquartered in the Mosque of Al-Aqsa in the area of Solomon's Temple. In Acre there was the Order of the Teutonic Knights which was composed of Germans. These Orders often flouted the authority of the Crusader Kings of Jerusalem. Since they were so bountifully subsidized by the kings of Europe, they soon amassed not only great wealth but enormous strength and independence as well.

SALADIN

Not unlike the days of the Bible, the Holy Land once again became a battlefield for conflicting power interests. In 1174, when Salah-e-din – or Saladin, as he is known to Westerners – became the ruler of Egypt, he successfully sought to gain control of Syria and Iraq too. The Crusader Kingdom of the Holy Land was caught in a vise, encompassed by a most powerful enemy on all sides. After some preliminary battles, the last and fateful encounter with Salah-e-din took place near Tiberias on the fields of the Horns of Hattin. The fragment of the "true Cross," which the Crusaders had carried into battle, was lost to the conquering Saracens. Their fifteen-thousand-man army was almost completely murdered or taken captive and enslaved. In the wake of the almost total annihilation of their principal source of defence, the castles and forts of the Crusaders remained virtually unmanned and slowly in unending onslaughts fell to the overwhelming odds of Saladin. Acre, Jaffa, Ashkelon were subdued and fell; and soon thereafter the capital of Jerusalem too. Saladin spared the lives of the Christians living in these places, even though he showed less compassion and concern for their Jerusalem churches, most of which he promptly converted into mosques.

The Crusaders continued to maintain their foothold in the land by retaining the coastal city of Acre. But even this redoubt was not held much more than a century. The Mamelukes, or "slaves," now came upon the Palestine scene. These were people of Turkish or Circassian origin who were to rule the Holy Land, Egypt, and Syria for the next 250 years. In 1291, they captured Acre, and put an end forever to Crusader power in the Holy Land.

At the beginning of the thirteenth century, Francis of Assisi founded his renowned order, the Franciscan Fathers. After his visit to the Holy Land, his monks began to establish themselves there. But it was not until 1342 that Pope Clement VI granted them full rights as "the Custos," the Custodians for the Roman Catholic Church of the Christian holy places. The Franciscans, despite the difficulties imposed upon Christians by Muslim authority, continued to welcome pilgrims, built hospices for pious visitors, and in general acted as the link between the Holy Land and the Western world throughout stormy and difficult centuries.

THE OTTOMAN TURKS

Almost to the day, the Ottoman Turks ruled over the Holy Land for four hundred years – from 1517 until 1917, when General E. H. Allenby's British forces marched into Jerusalem to proclaim the utter defeat of the Turks. All through the Ottoman period, a tug-of-war was waged between the Latins and the Greeks over their respective rights at the holy places. Both groups were principally concerned with the religious sites in and around Jerusalem and Bethlehem, but their interest also extended to other sacred sites, which each wished to place under its own separate jurisdiction. In addition, throughout the period, new churches and monasteries were built by both groups, some at ancient sites which they continually sought to revivify.

Legally, the status of the Christian communities remained unchanged for four centuries. Under the Ottomans, the religious communities of the Holy Land were stabilized and organized in what is known as the "millet system" whereby each recognized group is afforded internal autonomy in matters of religious preference and personal status. In these areas, the recognized religious communities were sovereign, and their own courts of religious or canon law were granted special jurisdiction.

But in spite of what seemed to be a just relationship, the Greeks had a special position. Among the Christian subjects in the Ottoman Empire, the Greeks were the best educated and the most influential, so they enjoyed a special and privileged status among the Christian communities at the Court of the Porte at Constantinople. Thus the Greek Christians could make their weight felt at the holy places. Indeed, at the very beginning of the nineteenth century, most of the fifteen thousand Christians living in the Holy Land were Greek Orthodox. The Russian Orthodox too, although defeated in the Crimean War, strove to maintain their prestige in the Holy Land, and during the last half of the century built many churches, hostels, and religious institutions in the land.

PROTESTANTS AND ANGLICANS

Until the first decades of the nineteenth century, Protestant contacts with the Holy Land were tenuous and minimal. American, British, German, and Swiss Protestant missionaries began arriving in some numbers toward the middle of the century. Both Anglicans and Protestants were seriously handicapped, as compared with the Catholic and Orthodox churches, the veteran groups in the East, for within the Ottoman Empire they enjoyed no legal status. To overcome this problem, Frederick William IV of Prussia conceived a plan whereby an Anglican bishopric in Jerusalem would be established to which other Protestant congregations could be affiliated. This "union" of the Lutheran Church and the Church of England in Jerusalem did not last very long – a mere forty years. Thereafter, each denomination went its own way.

In Jerusalem's walled city, Christ Church (Anglican) with a hostel and a school, was consecrated in 1849, and in 1898, outside of Jerusalem's walls, the Church of England opened its St. George's Cathedral and school. By this time an Arab section of the Anglican church had come into being, with its own priests and teachers, and it came to be known as the Arab-Episcopal Church.

The German influence continued to grow apace within the country. In addition to several new churches, the German Protestants made a very unusual contribution to the land. In the middle of the nineteenth century, a pietistic movement had begun in the South German city of Württemberg, as a secessionary splinter from the Lutheran Church. Its leaders called their movement *Der Temple*, the Temple, and they journeyed to the Holy Land to await the Second Coming. They became a very constructive element. Known as the Templars, they founded successful agricultural villages, and in the major cities they constructed their own residential suburbs.

THE LAND TODAY

Today, the Holy Land may serve as an international centre of inter-religious understanding and co-operation. Despite the strife and rivalry of the centuries, it is possible that, with the aid of the new and fresh winds of the ecumenical movement within Christendom, some of the antagonisms that have characterized the rival Christian claimants to the holy places in the past may soon be forgotten. Moreover, while suspicion and misunderstanding presently exist between the Arab and Jewish communities in the Holy Land, the day of a new *rapprochement* between them may yet dawn, bringing with it some of the splendour of the Golden Age which, in Spain, resulted in broad cooperation between Muslims and Jews for over five centuries.

Today, in the State of Israel, some 400,000 Arabs reside, 300,000 of whom are Muslims. Some ninety mosques are available, and more than two hundred Muslim clergy officiate. Muslim trustee-ship committees attend to the community's religious affairs and administer its religious endowments, known as the *wakf*.

Some seventy-two thousand Christians, mainly Arabs, also reside within Israel. And they belong to thirty different denomi-nations. Aside from Jerusalem and its holy places, in other parts of the land there are some four hundred churches and chapels, attended to by over twenty-five hundred clergy. The largest number, some twenty-five thousand, are Greek Catholic; there are also about twenty-two thousand Greek Orthodox, and about sixteen thousand Christians affiliated with the Roman Catholic Church, known in the Holy Land as the Latin Church. In the West Bank area – principally in Ramallah, Bethlehem, Beit Jalla, and Beit Sahour –there are about thirty thousand Christians.

There are also Druze, who broke away from Islam in the eleventh century, and who have since remained an indepen-dent and separate religious group. Some thirty-three thousand reside in eighteen villages in the Galilee and the Carmel areas. And in Haifa, the Universal House of Justice serves as the World Centre of the Baha'i faith which had its origin in Persia. There is probably no other region of the world where so many different religious styles and histories fit together in such close proximity. The very buildings – be they temples, churches, synagogues, mosques; walls, wells, or sepulchres – are living witnesses to the ecumenical fact that the great religions of the world can deem the same places sacred, and in the process can learn how to respect one another and co-exist creatively.

In the waters of the Jordan, near the Franciscan chapel not far from Jericho, a child is about to be baptized by monks from the chapel in a rowboat marked "Terra Santa" – "Holy Land."

The Abyssinian Church, whose liturgy is sung in the Geez language, is a Monophysite church of early Eastern origin. The presiding bishop is seen officiating here. There is a quaint chapel on the roof of the Holy Sepulchre.

The largest Christian group in the Holy Land is the Greek Orthodox, totalling some 70,000 souls in both Israel and Jordan. Their Patriarch is seen here at the head of a religious procession about to enter the Church of the Holy Sepulchre.

Outside the Church of the Holy Sepulchre the Greek Orthodox bishops participate in the ceremony of "Washing of the Feet" on Holy Thursday.

137

Armenians have been in the Holy Land since earliest times. They share rights with the Latins and Greeks in the Holy Sepulchre. Seen here is their Jerusalem church, St. James Cathedral, one of the most ornate and richly decorated Christian churches in the Holy Land.

"The Monastery of the Cross," called after its Arabic name, *Deir al-Musalliba*, graces one of "modern" Jerusalem's most beautiful valleys. It has, indeed, given its name to this fertile, olive-studded vale, the Valley of the Cross.

Greek Orthodox tradition traces this site to the time of Helena, mother of Constantine, who was said to have built one of Jerusalem's first monasteries on this place. Many legends abound about this picturesque area; according to one of them, Lot planted a cedar, cypress and pine here, and these grew into a single tree from which the "true cross" of the Crucifixion was later fashioned.

Until the nineteenth century, when it was turned over to the Greek Orthodox Patriarchate of Jerusalem, the monastery had served as the focus of pilgrims from Georgia in the Caucasus, which, like Armenia, had been a Christian Kingdom since the fourth century, with strong ties to Jerusalem

The Latin Church – as the Roman Catholic Church is known in the Holy Land – is largely administered by the Franciscans. Here, atop Mount Tabor, one of the highest points of the land, is their Church of the Transfiguration. A very old tradition going back to Apostolic times has it that Jesus was transfigured on Mount Tabor. In the foreground are the ruins of a medieval Benedictine chapel; in the background the hills of Galilee.

Shivta, or Subeita, was one of the six Negev cities south of Beersheba which the Byzantines had made part of Palestine. These towns were originally built by the Nabateans, a Semitic tribe which moved north from Arabia. A trading as well as an agricultural people, their conquest of the desert, by the end of the fourth century B.C., had transformed the arid expanse of the Negev into "the Suez Canal" of the ancient world.

Shown here are remains of the Centre Church, one of the three Byzantine churches built in the fifth and sixth centuries in Shivta. Some time after the Arab conquest of Palestine in the seventh century, a mosque was built on this very site, with its *mihrab*, or prayer niche, facing Mecca.

In the heart of the southern desert stands Avdat, which was also a Nabatean-Byzantine Negev city. Called after the Nabatean King Obodas, Avdat fell to the Romans very early in the second century. In the fifth and sixth centuries, an important monastery and churches were already there, combining the attributes of the settled city community together with the life of the desert.

Using the agricultural techniques pioneered by both Nabatean and Byzantine dwellers of desert Avdat, the "farmlands" of ancient times have come to life again, with the very same crops being grown by botanists from the Hebrew University of Jerusalem. In the background are reconstituted dams which channel the sparse rains and the sporadic flash floods from the surrounding slopes to the fields below.

Mar Saba, or St. Saba, the great monastery in the Wilderness of Judaea, is the home of monks who live almost completely as recluses and hermits.

Julian Saba, a fourth-century Syrian ascetic, came from Cappadocia to Palestine and founded four anchorite monasteries. These follow the style of the *laura*: a row or cluster of solitary cells around a common centre, which is used on Sundays for worship and sometimes on Saturdays as well.

Mar Saba is fantastically perched atop a steep slope of a wild gorge at Wadi en-Mar. The dome of Theoktotos – the Church God Built – is in the right centre, with the cupola of Saba's tomb seen to its left. Women are strictly prohibited from entering this monastery, but they may view it from the "Women's Tower" outside the monastery's walls.

In anchorite monasteries only one or two meals, usually Saturday and Sunday, are taken together. The Refectory, seen here, is more than a dining hall. Part of its function, too, is to serve as a bakehouse from which the monks take the bread to their cells, which with water, may often serve as their principal fare for the rest of the week.

A monk at Mar Saba, opening the door for infrequent visitors.

A monk at prayer in the desert.
The Monastery of St. Theodosius, in the Judaean Desert, is for cenobite monks, who live together as a community. Born in Cappadocia in 432, Theodosius came to Jerusalem as a young man and was received as a novice in a convent near the Tower of David. He left Jerusalem for the Wilderness of Judaea, taking the road out of Bethelehem toward the Dead Sea. There, on a mountain, he found the cave where tradition claims the Wise Men, when leaving Bethlehem, had stayed for the night. Theodosius settled there and with companions built some cells out of which, in the course of time, a great convent grew. It became a small city, with its pilgrim house, a house for the sick, lodgings and workshops for its monks, who, it is said, once numbered almost seven hundred.

Here we see heaped-up, neatly arranged skeletal remains of monks in the communal ossuary-cemetery at St. Catherine's Monastery in the Sinai Desert. The remains of archbishops and high-ranking clergy are placed in closed coffins and entombed in rock wall graves. The skeletal remains of all the other monks who have lived at the Monastery are put together, in symmetrical order.

This arrangement is prevalent in several other monasteries in the Holy Land. Monastics believe that in this way they are fulfilling the vision of Ezekiel's prophecy concerning the Valley of Dry Bones, as described in his thirty-seventh chapter.

The port of Acre has a long and checkered history. Known as Akko in Scriptures, it is one of the world's oldest cities. It lies at the tip of a wide crescent that sweeps southward toward Haifa and Mount Carmel. In the New Testament (Acts 21:7), Paul refers to Acre as Ptolemais, the name given to the city in the third century B.C.

Acre became the capital of the Crusader kings after they lost Jerusalem to Saladin in 1187, until in 1291 it, too, fell, putting an end to Crusader rule in the Holy Land.

In 1775, Ahmed al-Jazzar became the Turkish High Commissioner in Acre, and he built the beautiful mosque at the sea-wall, seen above, which still bears his name. After conquering Egypt, Napoleon tried to take Acre in 1799, but he failed, and his dreams of an eastern empire were thus ground into dust.

The Crypt of St. John in Acre in a recently excavated thirteenth-century Crusader palace, on whose foundations the Turks had built the fortress-like Citadel in the eighteenth century.
We note here the typical vaulted ceiling of Crusader architecture in the Knights' Hall of the palace built by the Hospitallers.

A new Christian Church School, recently built in the Galilean village of Rama. Inhabited mostly by Christian Arabs, but also by Druze, Rama's new church school is typical of the many new religious buildings Christians have been building in the Holy Land, not only to preserve the past and to call ancient places and events to mind, but also to provide for the religious growth and inheritance of their children.

150

In an Arab village school in the Galilee, a Roman Catholic nun teaches reading and writing.

Atop Mount Carmel in Haifa a Sunday Service for Christian scouts in an improvised outdoor chapel. The old is blended with the new.

The beautiful golden dome of the Baha'i Shrine dominates the middle-town of three-tiered Haifa and overlooks the Mediterranean. Baha'i is a world-faith which emanates originally from Persia. It has made Haifa its world centre. The Persian government persecuted the Baha'is, and their founder Mirza Ali Muhammed, or Al Bab, was shot in public in 1850. In 1909 his followers brought his remains to this site in Haifa for re-interment.

Still another splinter religious group which emanated from Islam is the Druze faith. All Druze have Arabic as their mother-tongue and almost all dwell in rural areas. The Druze religion began in Egypt sometime in the eleventh century. Today the largest number live in the Lebanon and Syria, with many thousands in Israel as well.

Indeed, Israel is the site of one of the holiest shrines in Druze religion – the Tomb of Nebi Shueib, or Jethro, father-in-law of Moses. It is located near Tiberias in Lower Galilee, and each spring, thousands of Druze flock to pay homage to this ancient Midianite leader, who has also been given a prominent place in the Koran.

Near Nebi Shueib's tomb, Druze enter their prayer-house, the *Kilveh*, for public devotions. Non-Druze are strictly forbidden to enter, as they are also prohibited by Druze tradition from being taught the secrets of the religion. Here, in a rare photograph, Druze are seen inside the *Kilveh*, adjacent to the Tomb of Jethro.

153

From the bell tower of the Holy Sepulchre in Jerusalem can be seen the minaret of a nearby mosque. The church calls its faithful to worship by tolling its bells.

But the mosque relies upon the *Muezzin*, from atop its minaret, to sing out his unique call to worship. Here he is, across from the Holy Sepulchre, chanting his invocations.

The Via Dolorosa.

Part Four: Islam in the Holy Land

THE FIRST ARABS

One or two centuries before Islam, Arabs had only a hazy knowledge of their ancestral origins. They had some recollection that in the ancient past there had existed several Arab peoples of whom they knew nothing at all. These they called *al' Arab al-ba'ida*, "the Arabs who had disappeared." These ancient peoples had first appeared on the stage of history in Syria, Iraq, and Yemen, but later were engulfed by the higher civilizations surrounding them.

That the Arabs and the Jews have roots in common, however, cannot be denied. To be sure, there is no record in the Bible that Ishmael, brother of Isaac and son of Abraham, was considered to be – what some have insistently called him – the "father of the Arabs." Ishmael was clearly a member of a most ancient tribe which soon vanished from the face of history. In the Bible, the term "Ishmaelites" is used as a common noun denoting a desert people of camel-breeders.

Nevertheless it was the Jews who first called the Arabs "cousins" and regarded them as children of Ishmael, the son of Abraham. It is a most interesting twist of history that this Jewish notion was later taken over by the Arabs themselves; it was Mohammed who made this point a cornerstone of his new faith. In the Koran, the Muslim Scripture, Mohammed had Ishmael help his father, Abraham, convert the pagan Ka'aba of Mecca into a shrine of the one true religion. Thus Mohammed claims that Abraham, the presumed physical ancestor of the Arab people, is the actual founder of Islam, their religion, as well. (Koran, Sura 2, Verse 125)

Moreover, the whole of the Koran seems pervaded by the spirit and person of Moses. The very idea of Moses – a Prophet with a Book – seems to have become central to the thought of Mohammed. Indeed, in the earliest days of his career, Mohammed knew only about the existence of one prophet, Moses, and he clearly regarded himself as his *bona-fide* successor. Thus he says: "Before this book there was Moses' book . . . and this book confirms it in the Arabic language." (Sura 46, Verse 12) "We have heard a book which came down from Heaven after Moses to confirm its predecessor." (Sura 46, Verse 29)

ARABS AND JEWS

Israel was an agricultural nation whose forefathers were farmers or at most semi-nomads in a region of an ancient, settled civilization. Northern Arabia, on the other hand, was the home of nomadic wanderers – Bedouins and traders. What then accounts for the great resemblances between Arabs and Jews? The resemblances are also reminders of the differences.

According to Genesis, Abraham, the founder of the Jewish people, was not only the father of Ishmael but also the founder of many other tribes that dwelled in Northern Arabia, and even as far away as Sheba in Southern Arabia. Abraham had sent his sons into the countries of the East, after giving them presents, leaving Isaac as the sole heir to the Land of Canaan. (Genesis 25:1-6) Some branches of Abraham's family, such as Lot and Esau, moved on to the arable lands in the east and south, while others, the Ishmael and Midian tribes, followed the great caravan routes which led out of Beersheba, eastward and southward.

There, these children of Abraham probably married the local tribesmen, and soon became what the Bible portrays them to be – the traders and the raiders of the desert and its fringes.

Most scholars believe that the emergence of a separate Arab people out of these earliest origins came only in the latter part of the second millenium, with the domestication of the camel. *Bedou* in Arabic means "outside," and the Bedouins were those who lived far away, outside the settled areas occupied by the sheep-and-cattle-raisers. It is only far out in the desert that good camels can be raised. These Bedouins, the early Arabs, were related to Abraham, to be sure, but they had moved into the desert. In many ways, thereafter, the Arabs remained a desert people, while Jews lived within settled areas.

MOHAMMED

Not very much is known about the ancestry and early career of Mohammed. Sometime between 570 and 580 he was born in Mecca and raised there by his grandfather as a poor orphan. Marrying Khadija, an older widow of a rich merchant, he was able to acquire wealth and position. The "call" came to him when he was approaching his fortieth year. But how, indeed, did he acquire his spiritual sensitivity, and what influences had reached him in determining the religious vocation that was to be his?

The Muslim tradition informs us that Mohammed was illiterate; he could not have read the Bible. Yet the very ideas of monotheism and revelation which permeate the Koran are distinctly biblical, and the influence of the Biblical stories – both Old and New Testaments – upon his own narratives is clear and unmistakable. It may very well be that his own knowledge of the Bible was imperfectly acquired from such second-hand sources as Jewish and Christian traders and travellers who came to the commercial centre that Mecca surely was. Or it may be that his spiritual origins can be found among the Hanifs, a pagan people of Mecca, who were opposed to the prevalent paganism of their compatriots and were seeking a higher form of religious expression, but were yet unprepared to accept either Judaism or Christianity.

His new teaching met with no opposition from local Meccans as long as they thought of his words not as the beginning of a new religion but rather as an Arabic-version of religious teachings prevalent among other peoples. Soon enough, however, he openly attacked the existing religious institutions of Mecca, and this brought upon him the wrath of the ruling class. He now turned elsewhere to seek a territory more open to his new faith: Islam, "surrender" to God. It was to Medina, a city some 280 miles to the north, settled originally by Jewish tribes, that he now turned his attention. There the Jews still maintained an uneasy balance of power in the midst of constantly warring, rival Arab tribes.

Mohammed's migration from Mecca to Medina is called the *Hijira* in Arabic, and it marks a crucial turning-point in his life and in the history of Islam as well. For this reason Muslims took the year 622, the date of the *Hijira*, and made it the starting-point of their calendar, just as Christian chronology was made to begin with the birth of Jesus. Medina made all the difference to Mohammed and to his faith. In the words of one scholar: "In Mecca, Mohammed was a private citizen, in Medina the chief magistrate of a community. In Mecca he had to limit himself to more or less passive opposition to the existing order, in Medina he governed. In Mecca he preached Islam, in Medina he was able to practise."

RELIGIOUS DUTIES OF ISLAM

Islam prescribes five specific religious duties, and these are incorporated into the *al-Arkan*, The Five Pillars.

The first duty is the Repetition of the Creed: *"La ilah illa Allah; Muhammed rasul Allah."* "There is no god but Allah; and Mohammed is the Prophet of Allah." The complete and unreserved acceptance of this confessional of faith and its frequent and faithful repetition constitute the first steps in the religious life of the Muslim. These simple declarations are heard throughout the Muslim world, and they pierce the air, as if trumpeted from the heavens above, in the muezzin's call to prayer, heard five times each day.

The religiously observant Muslim is a prayerful man, and prayer five times each day is the second of the religious duties of Islam. The first comes at dawn, the second at midday, and the last three at mid-afternoon, sunset, and nightfall. The faithful Muslim bows down toward Mecca, and usually offers up these words from the first chapter (or Sura) of the Koran, words that have been called by Christians "The Arabian Lord's Prayer."

"Praise be to God, the Lord of the worlds!
The compassionate, the merciful!
King on the day of reckoning!
Thee only do we worship, and to thee do
    we cry for help.
Guide thou us on the straight path,
The path of those to whom Thou hast been
    gracious: with whom
Thou art not angry, and who go not astray."

It is on Fridays that the faithful men gather for public prayer, usually assembling in the paved courtyard of the mosque at noon under the leadership of the *imam*. When women attend, they either stay behind screens or they sit in a separate women's section of the mosque. At the call of the muezzin, the men gather in the courtyard. They leave their shoes at the mosque's entrance and make their ablutions at the fountain – hands, mouth, nostrils, face, forearms, neck, feet. Entering the mosque, they sit for a few moments to hear a "reader" recite from the Koran. On the appearance of the *imam*, they take their places in long rows, facing Mecca, spaced sufficiently to allow them to throw themselves forward in prostration on their prayer mats or rugs. The *imam* recites all the prayers, and the worshippers silently and all as one follow him in his motions. When he stands erect they stand.

When he inclines his body and head, or drops to his knees, placing his hands on the ground in front of him, and putting down his forehead in "prostration," they do all these things the same moment that they see him do them. The standing posture, alternating with kneeling and prostration, accompanied by recitations from the Koran of adorations and praises of God – all of these are pervaded by a profound devotion. Throughout, the face is turned toward Mecca. After prayers, the *imam* usually preaches a sermon dealing with Islam, the Koran, or some topical subject.

The third religious duty is almsgiving. It is called the *zakat*. In the early days of Islam, this was a yearly tax paid either in money or in kind by every Muslim on his property or income. Gathered in by community officials into a common treasury, it was later distributed as charity to the poor, as well as given to *imams* and mosques for expenses and maintenance. Today, however, the *zakat* is considered a voluntary charitable gift, although in most regions of Islam it is universally practised.

Fasting during the sacred month of Ramadan is the fourth religious duty. All Muslims, except the sick and infirm, are expected to fast from dawn to sunset. Muslim tradition requires that no food or drink be taken as soon as it becomes possible to distinguish between a white thread and a black one at dawn, until at sundown the difference between the threads is no longer discernible.

A pilgrimage to Mecca, once in every Muslim's lifetime, is regarded as the fifth religious duty. Pilgrims, both men and women, are expected to be in Mecca – if possible, during the sacred month of Dhu'l-Hijja – in order to enter with thousands of other pilgrims into the annual mass observance of the circumambulation of the Ka'aba stone.

JUDAISM, CHRISTIANITY, AND THE PROPHET

When Mohammed first arrived in Medina, he had few followers. He hoped, however, to be accorded a most friendly welcome by the city's Jewish community. He felt that the Jews, to whose faith and Scriptures he felt so close, would receive him, as the Arabian Prophet, with understanding and open hearts. Indeed, in order to ingratiate himself to them, he adopted several specifically Jewish practices as his own, including the fast on the Day of Atonement and the recitation of prayer in the direction of Jerusalem. But Mohammed was terribly disappointed: The Jews of Medina did not accept him as a Prophet, and this caused him to drop the Jewish practices he had temporarily accepted, and in place of Jerusalem he substituted Mecca as the centre of his prayerful attentions. Indeed, he did this in a most interesting way. Even before Islam, the Ka'aba stone in Mecca had been the site of pagan Arab pilgrimage. Mohammed placed the seal of Islamic approval on the older pagan pilgrimage by announcing that it was Abraham and Ishmael, not the pagans, who had originally hallowed the spot and inaugurated the pilgrimage rites associated with it.

Slowly, however, his religion grew more and more Arab, and further away from Judaism and Christianity. With the adoption of the Ka'aba in Mecca as the central place of pilgrimage, the conquest of the city became a religious requirement. In 631, with the capture of Mecca, the immediate mission of Mohammed was completed, and after a short illness he died in 632.

Latent in the appeal of Mohammed was the drive toward unity – so urgently required by the Arabs of his day – which his religious teaching stimulated. There was also the need for a higher form of religious life than the widespread paganism which had been the life-style of Arabs until his arrival on the scene. True, his uncompromising monotheism, his insistence upon the "one true faith" – his own – had led to the erection of walls of separation between his followers, the Muslims, and the Jewish and Christian communities of faith. Nevertheless, his teachings were so completely dependent upon his Jewish and Christian predecessors that Muslims continued to venerate all of the major figures of the Old Testament, and to keep in high regard Jesus and some later Christian saints, particularly St. George.

As a result, travellers to the Holy Land are quick to note an amazing paradox. Many cenotaphs, memorials, and ancients sites sacred to Jews, because of Old Testament references, would probably have been lost were it not for the reverence shown these places by the Muslims who made them into holy places of their own. Moreover, the Hebrew and Arabic languages are related, both being Semitic tongues, and thus many of the ancient place names recorded in the Old Testament have been faithfully preserved by the Arabs, who gave the various towns and villages of the Holy Land where they resided following their conquest of the land, names that came straight into Arabic, out of the Hebrew original. As a result, archaeologists in search of the ancient places mentioned in the Scriptures are often directed to them not by any other homing device than the Arabic names they presently bear.

As early as 1841, the great pioneering archaeologists, Edward Robinson, described the methods he had adopted in seeking to identify the ancient sites which he investigated: "To examine everywhere for ourselves with the Scriptures (in Hebrew, Greek, and English) and apply for information solely to the local Arab population." The Arab names of places often contained at least an echo of the Biblical ones, and the topographical indications in the Bible often helped to confirm the identity of a site.

JEWISH ANTECEDENTS PRESERVED

As a result of such feelings of reverence toward many of the religious worthies of the Old Testament, places throughout the Holy Land preserved by Muslims have been kept available to Jewish religious pilgrims too. Some have also become sacred and venerable within the Christian tradition by way of the shared Biblical heritage. Without the Muslims, the ancient Well of Jacob in Shechem would long ago have been forgotten. But this very place, important to Jews, is perhaps even more important to Christians, for at that very well Jesus met the Samaritan woman. Clearly, this well could not have been kept intact were it not for the reverential attitude that the Muslims maintained toward the Old Testament patriarchs. Here, in this single site, is a typical, triple cross-reference: the well of Jacob, recorded in the Old Testament, referred to in another context in the New Testament, was preserved by the disciples of a third faith, the Muslims.

Without this Muslim predilection for keeping such sacred sites intact, many other places might very well have been forgotten or destroyed over the centuries. The tombs of the Prophet Samuel (Nebi Samwil), of the Prophet Jonah (Nebi Yunis), and of others are regarded as authentic by most scholars. Also, the various mosques which were established by Muslims on the very sites of ancient Jewish holy places have contributed to their safe-keeping. This is especially true of the Temple Mount which, in the hands of a conqueror less concerned with Old Testament and Jewish antecedents, could very well have been destroyed.

ISLAM AND CHRISTIAN SITES

Muslims, similarly, have deep respect for the person of Jesus, even though, as strict monotheists, they cannot accept the idea of the trinity or his divine lordship any more than can the Jews. As a result of serious clashes with Christians in the Holy Land, both before and during the Crusades, protracted periods of great tension between the two religious groups helped create antipathies. Yet, as with the Jews, Muslims continued to maintain living contact with the Christian tradition in the Holy Land, and have even "adopted" certain Christian saints as worthy of their profound respect. This is particularly true of St. George, patron saint of England.

St. George, according to Christian tradition, was born in the Holy Land, in the city of Lydda. While serving as a soldier in the Roman army, legend has it that he rose up, tore down the anti-Christian edicts of the emperor, and was martyred in the year 303. After his death, his remains were buried in Lydda which, for a time, was renamed after him – Georgeopolis. In the west, St. George is best remembered as a dragon slayer, who rode mounted high on his horse, lance in hand, ready to route the monster.

Muslims in the Holy Land have taken St. George into their tradition, and have made him one of their very own. Early and mediaeval Christians built many churches throughout the land to honour the memory of St. George, and at these very sites, Muslims invariably built mosques, or even took over Crusader churches, to give permanent tribute to *al-Khader*, the name they gave to St. George. In Arabic, this name means "eternal life," for *al-Khader* refers to green, living things.

Ruins of Byzantine churches, and later, of Crusader chapels and basilicas, also became favourite places for the building of mosques throughout the length and breadth of the country. To be sure, much of the motivation for this derived from a Muslim wish to root out the earlier religious undertakings of Christians and Jews. Yet there was also a feeling of relatedness on the part of Muslims to those Christian churches of the Holy Land that had been built in Byzantine and Crusader times to commemorate Biblical events or teaching. Because they possessed a wider view of history than only their own, Muslims helped Christians retain their ties to the older sites of the land by keeping alive memories of earlier times.

JERUSALEM – AL-QUDS

Al-Quds – "the Holy" – is the way Arab Muslims refer to Jerusalem. Jerusalem is not the holiest of Muslim cities; Mecca and Medina outrank it. But since the Dome of the Rock was built there, it became centrally associated with the developing Islamic tradition in the Holy Land.

Most historians now believe that this great Muslim sanctuary was not actually built by Omar Ibn al-Khattab, the second Caliph, who conquered Jerusalem and took it from the Byzantines, even though in popular reference it is often mistakenly called the Mosque of Omar. Rather, it was built at the order of 'Abdul-Malek Ibn Marwan, the Umayyad Caliph of Damascus, and was begun in the year 685 and completed six years later. Indeed, the Caliph's reasoning was said by one Muslim historian to follow such lines as these: "When the Caliph saw the Holy Sepulchre which is revered by the Christian world, he was afraid that this church would win the hearts of Muslims and so he decided to build a sanctuary even more beautiful." However, many contemporary scholars feel that the more probable reason for 'Abdul-Malek's building of the mosque was related to his own political not his religious thinking. 'Abdullah Ibn az-Zubeir had revolted against the Umayyads and declared the independence of Hejaz in the year 680, thus closing the area to the Umayyads. 'Abdul-Malek met this new and dangerous situation in an ingenious way: he created the mosque in Jerusalem as a place of pilgrimage, under his control, which could become an important centre of pilgrim interest, even if it would not outrank the Ka'aba in Mecca.

It was not easy to establish a new pilgrimage centre, and before proceeding 'Abdul-Malek was wise enough to consult the Muslim world. Reports vary about the response received to his appeal. Some say that the people accepted readily, but most accounts agree that it created great discussion and controversy among the Muslims. 'Abdul-Malek overcame the objections when he brought forth proof that the Prophet, while recognizing the value of prayer everywhere, encouraged Muslims to make a pilgrimage at any time they desired to the three following places: the Mosque of Mecca, the Mosque of Medina, and the Al-Aqsa Mosque.

Because of its many associations, the decision to build the new Mosque over the Rock was quite natural. When the Muslims had first occupied Jerusalem, they deeply reverenced the Rock because Mohammed had regarded it as holy, having its origin in Paradise. Soon tradition claimed it as the place from which Mohammed made his night journey to heaven, thus adding to its sacred character. The Rock had older associations as well. Muslims believed that Malki-Zedek, the Jebusite King of Jerusalem, had worshipped God and offered sacrifices there, and they regarded him as an ancestor.

They also followed a Jewish tradition which said that Abraham, the forefather of the Prophet, had offered his son Isaac as sacrifice to his God on the same spot, and that Jacob talked there to God and named the Rock "the Gate of Paradise." Solomon had built his Temple on it.

Four centuries later, in 586 B.C., the Temple was destroyed. The Second Temple, dedicated after the exile around 520 B.C., was replaced by the magnificent Temple of Herod the Great in 20 B.C. That, in turn, was demolished in 135 A.D. by Emperor Hadrian who erected in its place a pagan temple. This temple was still standing when Queen Helena came to Jerusalem in 335. Her Christian piety centred in Jesus, and she had no religious feelings concerning the ancient Temple. The site was deserted until it eventually became the city's dump heap; from the time of Helena's visit until the Muslim conquest of Jerusalem, the city's refuse was thrown there.

For many centuries the Dome of the Rock was erroneously called the Mosque of Omar. The mistake arose, no doubt, because Omar was associated with the early days of the Muslim conquest of Palestine, and because the record does show that he built a mosque soon after taking the city of Jerusalem. Arab historians believe that Omar Ibn al-Khattab, the second Caliph, who took Jerusalem from the Byzantines in 638 A.D., built his mosque in the area near the present mosque. He first consulted the Greek Patriarch, Sophronius, who took him to the Temple Mount, showed him the Rock covered with refuse, and assured him that it was the historical Rock and indeed a suitable place upon which to erect a mosque.

The fact that Omar himself helped clear away the filthy accumulations of the centuries and that 'Abdul-Malek Ibn Marwan made it the heart and centre of his beautiful sanctuary testify to the reverence they had for this ancient Rock. It has remained sacred in the Muslim world ever since.

THE GREAT MOSQUE

Even before the work was undertaken on the big structure of the Dome of the Rock, the first to be built was the Dome of the Chain to house the treasury. It also became the model for the larger, grander Mosque.

There are two circles of columns, eleven in the outer circle and six in the inner one, and all seventeen can be seen at one and the same time, from whatever side they are viewed. In the time of the Crusaders, the Dome of the Chain was made into a sanctuary dedicated to St. James, first Bishop of Jerusalem, but the name, Dome of the Chain, was derived from the belief that in the time of Solomon, a chain was miraculously suspended from heaven over this very spot. In any dispute, so the tradition had it, the chain would advance to meet the hand of the one who was in the right, but would swing away from the one in the wrong, eluding his efforts to catch and hold it.

It is not altogether certain where 'Abdul-Malek got the materials with which to build the magnificent sanctuary – whether from local sources or from abroad. Some believe he ordered that one of the beautiful domes of a Christian church in Ba'al-bek be taken down and transported to Jerusalem for use in the Mosque. Most scholars feel, however, that building material was plentiful in the country itself, even if only from the ruins of the Christian churches in and around Jerusalem destroyed by the Persians in 614.

As for the architectural style of the Mosque, here there can be little doubt that it was inspired by the original dome of the Church of the Holy Sepulchre. Nevertheless, the Great Mosque possesses an incredibly graceful dome, an octagonal shape that gives pleasure to the eye from every angle of vision, and symmetries so unusual they blend the architectural styles of the Byzantine, Persian, and Arab traditions into a harmony rarely matched in any building on earth. Indeed, many connoisseurs regard this Mosque as one of the most beautiful religious buildings in the world.

When 'Abdul-Malek was finished, about 100,000 golden dinars remained in the special treasury set aside for its construction. According to popular tradition, the Caliph offered the sum to the two chief engineers charged with the responsibility for the building. Both refused, saying, "We would rather give away our own money and the jewels of our wives than take this. It would be better to use the money to make the building more beautiful." It was then that 'Abdul-Malek gave the order for the gold to be melted and used to cover the dome. The Caliph also ordered a special cover, to be made of hair, wool, and leather, to protect the golden dome from the elements. He also arranged for curtains of brocade to be hung around the Rock from the Dome above, and the custom soon developed for the people to make circuits around the Rock.

AL-AQSA MOSQUE

In the earliest days of Islam, the name Al-Aqsa was applied to the entire area of the Haram-es-Sherif, but over the years it became identified with the mosque whose silvered-dome graces the southeastern part of the compound. It is, indeed, no less sacred than the Dome of the Rock, and while prayer services are almost never recited in the latter, five times a day, every day of the year Muslim prayers are offered in Al-Aqsa.

Some students are of the opinion that Al-Aqsa originally was the basilica built in honour of St. Mary by the Roman Emperor Justinian. Indeed, the mosque is arranged like a Christian basilica, except that it is in the shape of the letter "T" instead of a cross. On the important south wall, next to its renowned *minbar*, or pulpit, of ebony, ivory, and mother-of-pearl, are very special places of prayer, each of which relates to the older traditions of Judaism and Christianity. One of these is dedicated to Moses, Mussa, and the other to Jesus, Issa.

Al-Aqsa is large enough to hold more than five thousand worshippers at one time. Women foregather in the western aisle, while men pray apart from them, as in Orthodox Jewish worship to this day, filling the centre and eastern sections of the sanctuary. Before entering for prayer, worshippers make their ablutions at the large, iron-grilled water fountains which stand in the centre of the compound, midway between Al-Aqsa and the Dome of the Rock, and then remove their shoes, leaving them at the entrance doors.

There are altogether 155 windows in the building, 121 of which are of stained glass, fashioned in unusual arabesque designs. One of these, a remarkably beautiful rose-window, is probably of the Crusader period, and it serves as a living reminder and witness to the time the Knights Templar used the building for their own purposes. Indeed, below Al-Aqsa, there are large high, and extensive subterranean vaults popularly known as Solomon's Stables, which, legends claim, go back to his time, but whose present structure dates back only to the time of Herod. These stables were also used by the Knights Templar, and the holes which they employed for tethering their horses may still be plainly seen. Josephus, the Jewish historian of the Fall of Jerusalem, claims that when Jerusalem was besieged by the Roman Emperor, Titus, and before it surrendered in 70 A.D., large numbers of the city's population took refuge in Solomon's Stables, which can be reached today down flights of stairs from the east of the Al-Aqsa Mosque to its underground levels.

When the Crusaders occupied Jerusalem in 1099, they took over the Mosque and introduced many changes. They renamed it the Palatium, or Templum Solomonis, and transformed it into the headquarters of the Knights Templar. One part of the building they converted into a church, the other was made over to serve as their living quarters. They added some new buildings on the west side, and placed a double row of arches along the southern wall of the Haram. This addition was to serve them as their armoury, placed just above the underground stables, to which they put Herod's, if not Solomon's, engineering to early and repeated use.

THE LOVE OF JERUSALEM

True, Jerusalem did not lay claim to being Islam's holiest city. Yet the powerful hold it had had over the Jews and its central position in Old Testament history helped to give the city a very special place in the hearts of Muslims, too. In the writings of a tenth-century Arab Muslim, al-Muqaddasi – "the dweller in Jerusalem" – we find a statement of Muslim love for and attachment to al-Quds, Jerusalem the holy. It comes close to similar statements which can be found in mediaeval Jewish sources, panegyrics proclaiming the excellence of the eternal city:

"Neither the cold nor the heat is excessive here, and the snow falls but rarely . . . 'Just as is that [climate] of Paradise.' The buildings of the Holy City are of stone, and you will find nowhere finer or more solid construction. In no place will you meet with people more chaste. Provisions are most excellent here; the markets are clean, the Mosque is of the largest. The grapes are enormous, and there are no quinces to equal those of the Holy City. In Jerusalem are all manner of learned men and doctors, and for this reason the heart of any man of intelligence yearns for her. All the year round never are her streets empty of strangers. As to the saying that Jerusalem is the most illustrious of cities – is it not the one that unites the advantages of this World with those of the Next? . . .

As for the Holy City being the most productive of all places in good things, why, Allah – May He be exalted! – has gathered together here all the fruits of the lowlands, and of the plains, and of the hill country, even those of the most opposite kinds: such as the orange and the almond, the date and the nut, the fig and the banana, besides milk in plenty, and honey and sugar. And as to the excellence of the City! Why, is this not to be the place of marshalling on the Day of Judgment; where gathering together and the appointment will take place? Verily Makkah [Mecca] and Al Madinah [Medina] have their superiority by reason of the Ka'aba and the Prophet – The blessing of Allah be upon him and his family! – but in truth, on the Day of Judgment both cities will come to Jerusalem, and the excellencies of them all will be united."

Al-Muqaddasi complains of only one condition in his city. In his time, he writes, a good Muslim found life difficult in Jerusalem because the Christians and the Jews still had the upper hand in all affairs.

THE GOLDEN GATE

Perhaps nowhere else in Jerusalem do the three religions converge in so significant a manner as they do at the Golden Gate to the city walls. Although referred to as a single gate, it is in actual fact a double gate – the one on the south is called the Gate of Mercy, and the one on the north the Gate of Repentance. The older Jewish teaching had come to know God's presence as the *Shekhina*, the indwelling holy spirit, and it was believed that the *Shekhina* dwelled within the Holy of Holies, on the sacred rock. A later tradition, which came to the fore at the time of the Roman conquest of Jerusalem, projected the belief that when the Romans destroyed the Temple the *Shekhina* also departed from the Temple Mount, and went into exile with the Jews, leaving by means of the Golden Gate. It was then, too, that the tradition grew up that the sealed Gate of Mercy would not in any circumstance be reopened until the return of the *Shekhina* from its exile in the future Messianic age – entering the Temple Mount through the same gate through which it had first passed. In time, the belief also developed among Jews that happy people will go to Paradise through the Gate of Repentance, while the Gate of Mercy is to serve as a portal for the unhappy to go out to Eden.

The Golden Gate, as we have seen, had great importance for Christianity as well. During the Crusader Kingdom, processions from Bethany to Jerusalem on Palm Sunday had always entered the area of the Temple Mount through the Golden Gate. This was done in commemoration of the entry of Jesus into the city of Jerusalem at the beginning of Holy Week.

Islam, influenced not a little by older Jewish views, adopted its conception of mercy and repentance with some changes of its own. It held that the two divisions in the Golden Gate were made to commemorate the repentance of Adam and Eve for having disobeyed the orders of God in the Garden of Eden, while recalling the mercy God had offered the first couple as a free gift. In the Koran, there is reference to the need to separate the blessed from the damned, and the Golden Gate serves as the divider: Those to Heaven go out through one gate, those to Hell, through the other.

Still later, Muslims developed the belief – again based on variants of Jewish antecedents – that through these Gates all devout Muslims will pass along a narrow bridge, sharper than any knife, to the joys of Paradise to the east, across the Kidron Valley. Then, at the end of time, the closed gates will be reopened to permit pious Muslims re-entry across the sword-like bridge.

Indeed, just below the Golden Gates, Muslims eventually established their own cemetery, opposite the ancient Jewish cemetery across the Kidron Valley atop the Mount of Olives. By the ninth century, Muslims began to emulate the Jewish practice. Now they, too, began to bring their dead to the Holy Land to be buried, as Jews had been doing for many centuries. By the tenth century, the body of many a prominent Muslim was brought to Jerusalem for interment; by then, Muslims had incorporated the Jewish belief that the resurrection of the dead would take place in the Holy Land and in the Holy City at the end of days.

Jerusalem became for Islam and Christianty what it had been for the Jews – the symbol of future perfection, brotherly love, and peace. The prophetic, Messianic view which saw the city as a light unto nations, a beacon in the dark, and as a ray of bright hope amid the violent storms of life, has become the shared possession of these three great religions.

Some Arab communities still preserve many of their ancient ways. Here we see wheat being winnowed as it was in biblical times.

Bedouin men dance "the Debka" on festive occasions, in celebration of tribal joys.

A familiar pastime for Bedouin men is the "Fantasia," a rousing, shrieking sport played on horseback.

170

In the towns, ancient crafts like glass-blowing are still practised.

An Arab sieve-maker.

Inside the city walls of Jerusalem, an Arab market attracts the attention of passers-by.

Nebi Samwil, the Tomb of Samuel the Prophet. Muslims preserved this place throughout the centuries by erecting a mosque at the site. It stands tall on a high ridge overlooking Jerusalem. During the Middle Ages, Jews flocked to visit the tomb of the first of the literary prophets of the Old Testament, the prophet who had anointed Saul as Israel's first King. When the Crusaders came to the Holy Land they called this place Mount Joy, because from this special vantage point they had a rare first glimpse of Jerusalem.

174

An aerial view showing Jaffa Gate to the left and the Tower of David with its minaret in the right foreground. The golden Dome of the Rock is in the background, while the Mount of Olives can be seen on the horizon.

The Citadel, commonly known as the Tower of David, consists of five towers. The minaret to the right – the so-called Mosque-Tower – was added in the seventeenth century. Clearly visible are the four other towers, which, together with the mosque, make up the Tower of David.

The huge courses of masonry at the bottom of the Tower date from the time of Herod. He built a palace with three towers – one in honour of his brother Phasael, the second in honour of his wife Mariamne, and the third he named for his friend Hippicus. After the Muslim conquest of Jerusalem, the seat of government for some years was at the Tower of David.

Until the recent paving and landscaping of the area outside Jerusalem's city walls, the "Friday Market" was a typical sight. It was set up by Muslims from areas near Jerusalem to coincide with their weekly visit to the Great Mosque, Al-Aqsa.

Opposite page left.
The Pool of Siloam, built
by Hezekiah about 700 B.C.
to provide Jerusalem with
water, is still used by local
Arabs. The village nearby is
called Silwan, which helped
preserve the name by which
the Israelites had known it
– Shiloah.
The tunnel is one of the
great reminders of the
brilliant feats of engineering
performed by the ancients.
It flows for about 1600 feet
from the Spring of Gihon to
its outlet in the Pool of
Siloam.

Opposite page right.
In Sebastia, site of Israel's
ancient capital of Samaria,
we see an unusual site,
although one typical of the
Holy Land. A mosque is
found inside the compound
of a Crusader cathedral – a
Byzantine basilica built in
1165.

This page. Closeup of a
minaret, on the left, attached
to Crusader cathedral
remains at Sebastia.

At Sebastia, Judaism, Christianity and Islam have converged to recall with reverence the ancient worthies. The Tomb of St. John the Baptist in whose crypt the relics of St. John, as well as of the Hebrew prophets Elisha and Obadiah, were believed to have been kept, is also regarded as a holy place by Muslims.

The Monastery of St. Catherine, atop "Mount Sinai," the one seat of Christian worship in the deserts of Arabia. Paradoxically, within the walls of the convent there is also a mosque, which can be seen here. This is probably the only place in the world where a convent incorporated within its secretive compound a place of Muslim worship. Physically and symbolically, the place made sacred by Moses remains holy to Christians and Muslims, as well.

Prayers inside the Al-Jazzar Mosque, one of the largest and most important mosques within the State of Israel. Worshippers face the *mihrab*, the prayer-niche, in the direction of Mecca. To the right is the *minbar*, the ceremonial pulpit which is mounted by the religious leaders on Fridays, when sermons are customarily preached at the noon-hour Sabbath service.

The Nebi Musa procession from Jerusalem. The prophet Moses – Nebi Musa – is regarded by Muslims as one of their most significant figures. Mohammed regarded himself as a faithful, *bona-fide* successor to Moses. In the past, for about a week each year, great religious processions left Jerusalem to take part in solemn festivities at the very place Muslims believe is the Tomb of Moses, near the Dead Sea. Mount Nebo on the other side of the Jordan is visible from there. About 15,000 pilgrims, bearing festive flags, and many on horseback, have paid homage to Moses during the Feast of Nebi Musa.

Special prayers in honour of Nebi Musa take place in Jerusalem at Al-Aqsa Mosque, the Holy Land's most important prayer-centre for Muslims. Women may enter to pray in the mosque, but only in special sections. Many cannot enter for lack of space during occasions like Nebi Musa. Muslims pray five times daily facing Mecca, even when praying in Jerusalem. On this very spot, millenia before, thousands of Jewish pilgrims came to offer their sacrifices and prayers at the two temples which consecutively stood here. Since the eighth century, millions of Muslim pilgrims to Jerusalem have stood on the floor-stones of the Haram Compound to bring their fervent prayers to *al-Quds*, the sacred city of Jerusalem.

Here at Al-Aqsa, the women gather in the court separately.

This page.
Before work was begun in the seventh century on the great sanctuary, the Dome of the Rock, the Dome of the Chain, seen here to the right, was built to house its treasury. It soon became the model for the greater edifice, and is a replica in miniature of the larger building. There are two circles of columns, eleven in the outer circle, and six in the inner one, and it is virtually possible for all seventeen to be seen at one time from every angle of vision.

Opposite page left.
The steps to the Dome vary in width and height, and each flight ends in an elegant arcade called in Arabic *mawazeen*, or scales. The name is derived from the folk legend which suggests that the souls of men will be put on scales and weighed on the Day of Judgment. Here we see the Northwest *mawazeen*, with a view of the minaret known as *al-Ghawanmeh*, named after a noble family of Ghanim.

Opposite page right.
Upon entering any of the gates that lead to the Haram area, one walks some distance before reaching any of the eight flights of steps leading to the higher elevation on which stands the Dome of the Rock. Here we see the summer pulpit alongside the *mawazeen*.

Al-Aqsa, and not the Dome of the Rock, is the place for regular, daily prayer. Both occupy the area of the Haram Compound, and in the middle, the fountains for washing of hands and feet – ablutions before prayer – may be found.

186

The Golden Gate is actually a double gate with two separate divisions. Here, in a rare picture, we see it from inside the walls. On one side is the Gate of Repentance, on the other, the Gate of Mercy. Below this gate is the Muslim cemetery, dating back probably to the tenth century. Under the influence of Jewish teaching, Muslims at that time emulated Judaism, which had long before established a cemetery across the way, on the Mount of Olives, in order to make ready for the time of resurrection, and allowing the dead to be on hand to pass through the Golden Gate. Jesus, Christian tradition holds, entered the city through these gates on Palm Sunday.

Following page.
Jerusalem – old and venerable, beacon of hope even in the darkest of days. Synagogue, Church and Mosque rekindle their faith in peace tomorrow, if not today.

Conclusion: Tributes to the Land

The Lord said to Abram . . . "Lift up your eyes, and look from the place where you are, northward and southward and east-ward and westward; for all the land which you see I will give to you and to your descendants for ever. I will make your descendants as the dust of the earth; so that if one can count the dust of the earth, your descendants also can be counted. Arise, walk through the length and breadth of the land, for I will give it to you."

(Genesis 13:14-17)

By the waters of Babylon,
    there we sat down and wept,
    when we remembered Zion.
On the willows there
    we hung up our lyres.
For there our captors
    required of us songs,
    and our tormentors, mirth, saying,
    "Sing us one of the songs of Zion!"

How shall we sing the Lord's song
    in a foreign land?
If I forget you, O Jerusalem,
    let my right hand wither!
Let my tongue cleave to the roof of my
        mouth,
    if I do not remember you,
if I do not set Jerusalem
    above my highest joy!

(Psalm 137:1-6)

Palestine is the land in which the history of Israel has achieved, in the Person of our Lord, its aim and purpose for humanity. Consequently, as Jesus gathered up the significance of this land's history into Himself, it must have been an appropriate place for the upbringing both of the People of God and the Son of Man . . . one familiar with Palestine realizes that Jesus cannot be fully apprehended apart from her; for the Child was the gift of God to her. His life-work was in the first place to be not only *in*, but also *for*, this land.

Gustaf Dalman

Remember Moses said
   To his people: "O my People!
   Call in remembrance the favour
   Of God unto you, when He
Produced prophets among you,
Made you kings, and gave
You what He had not given
To any other among the peoples.
O my people! enter
The holy land which
God hath assigned unto you,
And turn not back
Ignominiously, for then
Will ye be overthrown,
To your own ruin."

(Koran: Sura 5, Verses 22-23)

In beloved Jerusalem, where three great religions meet, prayer and meditation for hopeful tomorrows.

When the Muslims occupied Jerusalem they came with a spirit of reverence for the Rock because Muhammad had said that the Rock of Jerusalem was a holy one, having come from Paradise. Tradition soon claimed it as the place from which Muhammad made his night journey to heaven, thus adding to its sacred character. They believed that Malki-Sadek, the famous Jebusite king of one of the earliest tribes to enter Palestine from the Arabian Peninsula, worshipped God and offered sacrifices there. They also believed that Abraham, the forefather of the prophets, had offered his son Isaac, as a sacrifice to his God on this same spot; that there Jacob talked with God and named the Rock "The Gate of Paradise."

Aref Al-Aref

Index

Grateful acknowledgment is made to
the following for permission to use the
photographs in this volume:

Elia Photo Service, Jerusalem
Government Press Office of Israel,
    Tel Aviv
Israel Museum, Jerusalem
The Shrine of the Book, Jerusalem
Foto Custodia Terra Santa, Jerusalem
Garo Photo Studio, Jerusalem

The Revised Standard Version of the
Bible has been followed in all biblical
quotations.